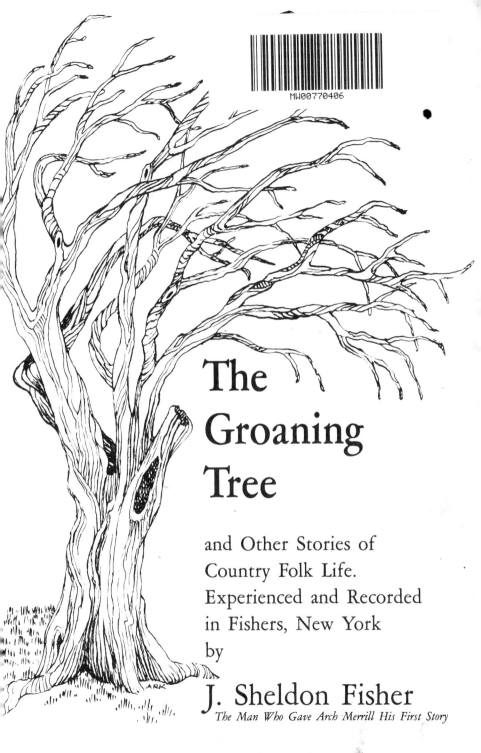

The Groaning Tree

and Other Stories of Country Folk Life. Experienced and Recorded in Fishers, New York by

J. Sheldon Fisher
The Man Who Gave Arch Merrill His First Story

Empire State Books—Interlaken, New York—1987

First Printing — December 1987
Second Printing — June 1994

Manufactured in the United States of America
Library of Congress Catalogue Number 87–23290
ISBN: 0–932334–95–4

A *quality* publication of
Heart of the Lakes Publishing
Interlaken, New York 14847

Dedication

To the newcomers of our communities.
That they will know that our area
is rich in folk history.

Contents

Introduction

As high-tech industries and subdivisions increasingly spread over the hills and into the valleys around the western New York community of Fishers in Ontario County, the legends and stories of succeeding generations which have flourished here for nearly two centuries are in danger of being lost forever.

Although anonymity now afflicts countless similar communities across the nation which have lost touch with their past, this need not now be the fate of Fishers. Moreover, other present and former rural communities can glimpse portions of their own past in this work, which records stories enacted with slight variations in many other localities.

Since boyhood I have been intrigued with the local folklore. I was born in the homestead built by my forebears in 1811. The death of my father when I was ten caused me to listen especially closely to the recollections of older family members. As I grew up in those years before television—and even radio—I also spent many hours listening to older neighbors as they told of earlier times. Thus now, in my eightieth year, I can not only look back upon my own observations and participation in events which date back practically to the beginning of this century and I can also remember accounts of others who told of their own experiences dating back to before the Civil War and who could repeat stories told by their own parents and grandparents thus extending the sources of this lore back to memories of those born prior to the close of the eighteenth century, the time of the first white settlement of western New York.

This collection of folk tales, as well as those in my other book, *The Fish Horn Alarm,* therefore tells of the days when the first mail carriers were chased by wolves, when bears stole pies from pantry windowsills, when the railroad came, the automobile arrived and, in more recent times, of incidents at the time of the opening of the New York State Thruway, which has been so influential in Fishers' growth as a high-quality residential, commercial and computer industry center, and in its becoming an integral part of suburban Rochester.

Beyond having ties with actual historical events, these stories provide windows into various stages of everyday life. They tell of Menzo's prize rooster, Henry Garling's mad cow, "Ett" Hill's fish horn alarm, and of the courtship of Helen Jane. At the other end of the spectrum they report tales of the ghost of Eliza O'Brien, train robberies, the murder of Elizabeth Woodin and atrocities of the Morrissey Gang of Poverty Huddle.

The settings of many of these stories are barely recognizable today. The railroad station is no longer the hub of the Fishers community. Indeed, both the station and the railroad itself are gone, leaving only the vacant cobblestone pumphouse built to serve woodburning locomotives as the reminder of Fishers' once-vital link with the outside world. The millpond also remains, but the mill does not. Jones' Hall has been converted into an apartment and the music of "Fiddler" Barry has been stilled.

Yet it is my hope that through these stories some of the flavor of Fishers' past may still survive, to entertain and also to inform persons who would otherwise follow unknowingly into the footsteps of those who were here before.

J. Sheldon Fisher
Fishers, New York

The Groaning Tree

Who ever heard of a tree groaning? One tree did give off such sounds—it attracted the curious for a number of years.

It was pictured in a newspaper series about Western New York curiosities. The publicity brought more visitors—many of whom became upset over the nerve-wracking groans.

This fabulous tree was a giant hollow elm estimated to have been over two hundred years old. It was located on the Woolston property just over the fence from the southwest corner of our farm.

Civil War veteran King Brownell, who operated the Fishers Mill, assured me that he had seen and heard groaning trees in his lumbering days. He said that it was not the same as heavily frosted trees which snapped and sounded like fired guns when the frozen sap expanded. Neither did it sound like tree limbs rubbing against each other making very loud squeaks. He dared me to find out why the tree groaned. Thinking that it would be quite an adventure, and with the help of my brother Francis, I prepared myself by filling my carpenter's apron with heavy spikes, a scout axe, knife and a flashlight.

At the base of the tree was an arched doorway; by a slight stoop one could walk into the hollow tree. Flashing the light upwards it reminded me of a farm silo although it was not as wide.

Since it was not possible to put up a ladder inside, I drove spikes on the inside for the 45 foot climb. The higher I climbed the closer I got to the groaning. It sounded as if someone had gotten stuck up there before me. Several times I felt like getting out. But if I had done so, I knew Old King would have a good laugh in public at my expense—he was very stoic when it came to pain. During the war his side was shot away. It seemed every bone in his body had been broken when his clothes were caught in a whirling mill shaft. Most of his fingers were cut shorter at one time or another. He kept the fingers in alcohol to be placed in his coffin when he died—and this was done. He didn't groan at severe pain.

I thought of his fearlessness as I climbed upwards and passed a den of baby racooons who had an outside entrance. I startled an owl which flew at me.

But it wasn't the owl which did the groaning. It was coming from an opening in a hollow limb. When the westerly wind hit the hole head-on it had the resonance of a bow being drawn across the strings of a bass viola.

This solved the mystery of the groaning tree to King

Brownell's satisfaction. Soon after, Jack Woolston had the tree cut down in order to avoid a possible lawsuit by an injured trespasser.

This discovery gave me an idea to give a vacant house a reputation of being haunted. The heirs to the McGovern house on Lower Fishers Road could not be located and squatters moved in and out. An open attic vent on the west side was just right for suspending empty ale bottles with the uncorked ends facing the wind. It was ideal—the moans and groans echoed through the empty house. Since headlights from cars coming around the corner would shine for a moment on the house, I lightly painted a phosphorescent figure on the side of the building. All of this apparently disturbed the overly superstitious and one day the house burned to the ground.

Robbery by a Snakehead

In August of 1845 an unusual combination of events happened, which created considerable excitement and speculation. On the curve just east of the Fishers Station a passenger train derailed.

The situation which caused the wreck was the same condition which had been causing wrecks on most railroads during the 1840s. The railroad tracks were nothing more than wooden rails with a narrow strip of iron spiked along the top of the wood. With many train wheels riding over the rails every day, spikes often would loosen and the ends of the straps would curl up and get tangled in the wheels. These were called "snakeheads."

There are numerous records of people being skewered and killed when the snakehead came up through the passenger coach floor. It happened on that day in August to the Auburn and Rochester Railroad passenger train. The iron track came up through, ripped a passenger seat off the floor and shoved it through the ceiling of the coach and out onto the ground. The wooden coach was pretty well demolished, but no one was badly injured. The passenger who was sitting in the damaged seat had nearly all his clothes ripped off.

According to my informant of many years ago, the passenger's name was "Jim" Harrell of Geneva, a courier for a Canandaigua bank who was headed for Rochester. He was carrying an envelope containing $2,500. When Jim was revived, he couldn't find his envelope. Even when the wreckage was cleaned up, they couldn't find it. It was then believed that he was robbed while he was unconscious, although his hand gun was not taken.

Next to the tracks on the west side was the home of Thomas Burns. The foundations are still visible. Mr. Burns had two pet crows. Crows are like packrats, for they will collect anything that amuses them. Sometime later, the robbery was solved when the envelope was found in the pet crow's nest with the money still in it.

Jim had been robbed by the crows with the snakehead as an accomplice.

The Hard-Working Ghost

Richard Hayes was the hardest working man in the Fishers area. He was grinding grain in his mill from before sunup until after sundown. He didn't seem to know when to quit. When he wasn't running his millstones, he was cutting wood. He worked so hard that he exhausted himself, and in 1816 he sold the mill after only six years ownership. However, he continued to live in the mill house until he died.

The house was rented in the winter of 1832–33 to the Reverend Phineas Howe Young, a brother of Brigham Young, who by that time joined the Mormons and went west.

The mill house today is known as "The Dutch" because it was later rented to tenants of German extraction. Many of those tenants honestly believed that Richard Hayes never left the place and was always doing something around the house.

A poltergeist spirit which moves things is often noisy and associated with misbehavior. The Old Dutch poltergeist was quiet and industrious, although at times facetious. Tools which were believed to be in the house were found in the barn and vice versa. A resident could never be sure that he would find what he wanted in the logical place. Sometimes it seemed that the spirit just wanted to tease the household. Articles were often removed and placed in ridiculous places. Items would disappear and then be returned after a lapse of time.

I tried to investigate this house on Main Street, near the

Monroe County line, about fifty years ago, in order to learn more about these strange happenings. The renters at that time were Mr. and Mrs. Charles Berendt, an immigrant German couple. I asked if they had had any experiences with ghosts in their house. They said, "Yes and plenty. Watch that empty chair for a few minutes." I did, and it slowly rocked.

I explained that a draft from the open door was causing it to rock. They closed the door, and it continued to rock. They said that the chair was in the house when they came and that they also were going to leave it when they moved out. Mr. Berendt said that he inquired of Jim Sullivan, who had owned the house, and was told that the chair had been left alone in the house for years.

I asked if the Berendts ever had any encounters with the poltergeist. He said that a couple of nights before, while he and his wife, Annie, were sitting quietly after supper, they heard the sound of sawing down cellar. When I asked him if he went down to find out who was sawing, he said, "Absolutely not." The next morning he did go down and found his wood all sawed and stacked. He added that when they got up in the morning they might find the kitchen kettles on the dining room table or the table spread out on the kitchen floor.

Old friends of mine later bought the house and I told them what to expect in order that they might not be too shocked when things were not normal. I soon got a call from them in much alarm. Their home was furnished with fine antiques. By the door they had placed a rare vase on a stand. They were deeply shocked one night when they came home to find the vase missing. Two months later they came home and found the vase back in place. After a few experiences like this, they learned to expect such irregularities.

Horse Thievery

The Horse with the Wiggly Ears

Some unusual things sometimes never make the newspapers. The horse with the wiggly ears did because it was stolen. The whole event, from the time of the theft to the recovery, made conversation for years afterwards.

Horse stealing was big business before the arrival of the automobile. The penalties were greater for stealing horses than automobiles, because the livelihood of farm families depended upon them. Professional criminals often organized to steal fine horses; horses stolen locally were often traced to distant cities.

The Fishers vigilantes were a good match for the horse thieves who dared to operate here—and many did. This organization was composed of most every person who owned horses. Dues collected would pay for a person's expenses to track down a stolen horse. The housewife was an important link in the organization. She usually had a good view of the horse pasture during the day, while the husband and hired men were alert during the night with the help of a good dog.

When horses were being stolen it was not always easy for one farmer to stop them, since the thieves often operated in a gang of three or four men. A signal system was designed which proved very effective. Each house had a dinner bell. Three strokes and a pause on a bell meant horse thieves. Each farm hearing the alarm bell would sound their own until all of the bells in the countryside were ringing. As many as could would get well-armed and wait along the roadside or at an intersection for the culprits to pass. When the thieves were intercepted, blasts on a conch horn or a bugle would give the location, and vigilantes from every direction would close in on the thieves. After the capture, the robbers would be roughly hogtied and taken to the Fishers Railroad Station and carted off to the Ontario County Jail.

Fishers Vigilantes in Action

On the Mendon Road, William Hill had a large farm where he raised excellent horses. One day his wife, Miranda Woolston Hill, discovered their horses being stolen. Being a good rifle shot, she wounded two of the horse thieves and stampeded their horse and buggy. She singlehandedly corraled the three horse thieves with her gun until help came.

Her sister's husband, George Washington Hill, who was also her husband's brother and lived at an adjoining farm at 7694 Main Street, Fishers, was not so lucky in saving his horses. It was a clean getaway with no traces. Sometime later Mr. Hill was in Buffalo on business and saw his favorite carriage horse being driven down the street. He had the driver arrested. The driver proved ownership to the judge, but Mr. Hill fought hard in claiming his ownership. He got the judge to agree to a novel idea: have the horse shipped back to Fishers station to see if the horse would go directly to its former home.

The stage was set and Hill's barn was left open. The situation attracted wide attention—the Fishers vigilantes gathered to meet the train containing the judge, jury, and interested lawyers from Buffalo. There was considerable doubt in the minds of the jury that the horse really did belong to Mr. Hill and the lawyer for the defendant was planning to seek a penalty against Mr. Hill for false arrest, if his scheme did not work.

The horse was taken from the train and was headed in the opposite direction from the barn. The horse whirled around and headed through the gauntlet of people towards the Hill farm. The jury began complaining that the horse had no choice but to stay on the road and go in that direction because of the crowd of vehicles west of the station. The road was lined with spectators and tension grew as the horse got nearer the barn. The constable cleared the people back in order to give the horse a choice of direction. It turned down the Hill driveway, into the barn and into the correct stall. A great cheer arose from the audience, for the horse had vindicated George Washington Hill.

A victory dinner was served on the back lawn of the Fishers Hotel. The Fishers vigilantes had been so sure that Mr. Hill was right that they had planned an old-fashion social for all of the

The Fishers Hotel operated by Homer J. Hill.

visitors, serving the food they had prepared. The hotel keeper, Homer J. Hill, exhibited some of his famous race horses outside of the livery stable.

Mr. Hill had recognized his horse on the Buffalo street by its unique manner of walking. When the horse's right foot went forward, the right ear would flop forward. The left ear was synchronized with the left front foot. When the horse speeded up, so would the ears flip-flop accordingly.

The horse became an instant celebrity and was exhibited at county fairs.

Mr. French's Horse

Shortly after the excitement about the stolen horse with the wiggly ears, Alexander Hamilton French on Malone Road had one of his valuable horses stolen. Photographs of the horse with its owner were posted in many places. Due to the conspicuous markings, the horse could be easily recognized and, therefore, hard to transport past watchful eyes. Because of this, it was reasoned that it had to be taken to a local hideout.

Wooded and rugged areas for miles around were searched by armed men on horseback. One area to search was a long wild, wooded ravine called the "Gulf." It is located on the far western end of the Stephen Van Voorhis farm on Fisher Road. That part of the Gulf, now a portion of a rest area on the New York State Thruway, was often referred to as "Rustler's Roost."

A posse of about 150 men on horseback from Mendon, Ionia, and Fishers formed a wide circle around the Gulf and worked towards the center. There in the natural amphitheatre were dozens of stolen horses. A ruckus arose from the stolen horses when they heard the posse's horses. They all began to whinny and six men came out of a shack with their hands up.

There, in this drove was the much sought-for prize brown and white horse. A crude attempt had been made to apply a brown dye to the white hair on the horse but rain had made the temporary coloring run.

The six men were hog-tied with ropes and loaded into a box car of a freight train headed for Canandaigua where they were put in jail. A spectacular trial put the men out of circulation for a long time.

This spectacular raid marked the end of organized horse rustling around Fishers. What happened to the horse thieves was well publicized, so the hazards were not worth it but because it was so isolated, the Gulf ampitheatre then became a center for illegal cock fights.

The horse stolen in 1885 from Alexander French by a gang of thieves who took it to Rustler's Roost. Mr. French, of Ionia, posted this photo in all public places to help apprehend the theives.

Snowbound

On a Saturday night in February, 1926, many residents from towns along the Auburn Road of the New York Central Railroad were on their way home from Rochester on what turned out to be a memorable weekend. The Auburn Road was well-known for being on time. The #2 train out of Rochester at 4:15 a.m. held the record of being the oldest train in the world on the same schedule.

Train #18 had to make connections at Canandaigua with the Pennsylvania and at Geneva with the Northern Central and the Lehigh Valley. The train consisted of a mail car, a baggage car, two passenger coaches, a New York Central small Pullman car named "Fishers" headed for New York City via Syracuse, and two red-colored Pullman cars, one named "Williamsport," headed for Philadelphia and Washington, D. C. On board also were many people who worked in Rochester and were coming home for the weekend along with the regular Saturday shoppers.

It was memorable because the #18 passenger train, which left Rochester about 7 p.m. that evening loaded with passengers, did not complete its schedule until three days later.

Everything was normal other than a mid-winter snow storm in progress. The control towers routed the train through the Rochester yards to the Auburn Road tracks at Brighton, where several passengers boarded. A stop was made at Pittsford, where several more took the Pullmans. Before the train left, the

Pittsford telegraph operator had received a message from Fishers that the storm was intense in this area with an unusually heavy snow. A check was then made with the train dispatcher to see if another locomotive should be added. It was found that no engine was steamed up so it could make the run on such short notice, and besides, the crews were home for the weekend.

The train proceeded on its way, rumbling over the canal bridge towards Hughes' Flats, the storm trap of generations of trains. While crossing this open stretch, it was questioned at times whether or not the train could make it. Rounding Baldwin's Curve, the Railroad Mills station came into sight. On board was the jovial overweight "Hank" Wallman, Auburn Road engineer, on his way home for the weekend. Number 18 was not scheduled to stop at this station on Saturdays but did so this time to get "Hank" nearer home because of the storm.

The storm had increased so much in intensity that it caused the locomotive a great deal of difficulty getting into motion for the mile up-grade towards Fishers. About 1000 feet from the Railroad Mills station the train plunged into a huge snowdrift and came to a stop. The starting and stopping with powerful lunges both ways seemed to only anchor the train more firmly. The drive wheels then spun only on one spot, burning depressions on the steel track. The engineer finally conceded defeat to the power of nature.

With all of the severe jolts, the passengers soon realized that they were going to stay right in that spot for some time and that they were hopelessly trapped. The train crew was upset because they could do nothing about it. The conductor and brakeman went through the cars and explained that it was going to be an all-night vigil.

The Fishers station agent, D. K. Brownell, was waiting for the train to arrive at the appointed time. "Hank" Wallman was reached by phone at his home and said that the train had left the Mills about a half hour before. This information was sent to the train dispatcher, who sent out a snow plow and rescue crew, which foundered on Hughes' Flats. This plugged the rescue attempt from the west. Rescue attempts from the east were just about out of the question, because the nearest plow was 90 some miles away in Syracuse. The railroad men knew that they were in deep trouble and expected a repetition of the snowbound passenger train, which was confined for two weeks on the Paddleford's curve near Canandaigua. The great snow storm of March 14, 1916, with 20 foot drifts, was not forgotten.

Back at the train near the Mills the engine had enough coal and water to keep up steam for heat and light for the emergency. Morning came. The impatient passengers could still hear the howling wind and were driven back into the cars by the blinding snow. Walking the aisles became a diversion which allowed the passengers to get acquainted and get exercise. Several of the Fishers people made it to the station from the train. The Fishers firemen and their wives prepared food, which was taken down the tracks on horseback. The story was that a baby was born on the train.

Morale was high. Several good entertainers were on the train. Irving Cline, noted musician and state champion fiddler from Phillips Road, and Jack "Fiddler" Barry from Fowler Street were there. They set up the baggage car as a dance hall. Charlie Fisher, prankster, story-teller, and entertainer, told some of the stories printed here.

All of us local lads were hired by the railroad to dig out the train after the storm subsided. Our first job, however, was to clear the snow from the switches at the station to make it possible to bring in rescue trains. After this we were hired by the town to dig out the heavy snow drifts on Wangum and Fisher Roads.

Old Car Escapades

The transition from the horse and buggy transportation to the motor car was tough on those people who were trying to adjust to it. "Giddyup" wouldn't start the old Model T Ford, nor would "Whoa" stop it. The automobile was not a year-round vehicle like the old, long dependable buckboard wagon. The Ford car with its high wheels was the outstanding car that could cope with the terribly rough roads and also go through fields if necessary.

The first Ford car agent in the area was Ambrose C. Ford of Fishers who was said to have been a cousin of Henry Ford. He started his agency in 1905 when he bought the first Ford car here. This was shortly after the Ford Motor Company was established in 1903. Ambrose and his brother, Charles, had established the properous Ford Seed Potato Company here in 1879; the car agency continued along with that business for 18 years.

The Ford car became a way of life here, but when winter approached, the car was jacked up on blocks until spring to take the weight off the tires and the water was drained out of the radiator. Automobiles created a new set of traveling rules and protections, which brought about new businesses. Dangerous shoulders and sharp curves along the country roads could be negotiated by horse and buggy, but not by the growing numbers of automobiles. Board fences offered no protection to a car slipping off the road. In 1910, J. Y. McClintock, Monroe County

Superintendent of Highways, patented a concrete guard rail to be used at dangerous highway spots.

A company to manufacture guard rails was formed with George L. Meade as president. A new factory was built in Fishers next to the Hill Sand and Supply Company. Production was started immediately and about 30 men were employed. The rails weighed 325 pounds each and the posts were 225 pounds. The cost of installation was rated at 7½¢ per linear foot when the price of labor was 22¢ per hour. The price of the guard rail was 70¢ per linear foot F.O.B. Fishers in freight car lots of 18 tons. With the construction of more state highways, cheaper guard systems were found and the Fishers plant was closed.

The owners of Ford cars had many tricks played upon them. When a car was parked, two men could lift up the rear and place blocks under the axle. Of course, the wheels would spin and not move the car. Farmers would jack up the rear of the car and with a belt around the wheel they could power farm tools for sawing wood and other chores. The Ford chassis was put to all kinds of uses. Leo Hunt and John Woolston rebuilt them into powered farm cultivators.

William Stanley bought a new Model T Ford. While taking it home, he couldn't stop it by yelling "Whoa!" He sheared off the top as he went under a low hanging apple tree limb. George Proseus, a regular Ford car driver, tried to drive his daughter's new Essex gear-shift car into the barn. What he thought was the peddle shift was instead the gas peddle and the car crashed right through the wall of the barn. We were eating dinner at the time and heard the loud crash and the splintering of timbers and saw the car protruding through the barn wall.

Herman Christian and Albert Kossow dared to drive their Ford car in winter to their work at the railroad car shops in East Rochester. Someone reminded them that springwater in creeks never froze and thus it would be good antifreeze in their radiator. However, to be on the safe side, they drained the water each night and replaced it with fresh creek water in the morning. One subzero morning the radiator water boiled out when near Irondequoit Creek. With his pail, Herman began to refill the radiator but he slipped on the ice and fell into the creek. Al went to pull him out and he, too, slipped into the creek. Finally, the radiator was filled and they drove on to work. When they arrived they were both frozen to the seat and couldn't get out. Their co-workers found a heated room in the shop, pushed the car in and thawed out the frozen riders. The lesson which they learned was that spring water would freeze like any other water!

Popular Art Lewis, when he was the Fishers postmaster, fire chief and ardent helper of woman and mankind, found that in being a good Samaritan strange things could happen to one. Catherine Bryant, a community leader, fell on the ice and broke her hip. The Canandaigua Hospital sent an inexperienced driver. In placing the ambulance in position to load the patient, the driver refused Art's advice and got the vehicle stuck on a patch of ice. The driver insisted on spinning the wheels at high speed. He was told that if he got traction at that speed he would snap the axle, and that is just what he did. Art found a chain and with his car he towed the ambulance the 15 miles to Canandaigua. The driver blew the siren constantly all of the way and into the city limits. A city policeman, upon hearing the siren and seeing Art's car continuously in front of the ambulance, stopped him and charged him with obstructing the passage of an ambulance. The policeman refused to believe Art until he tripped over the chain.

Menzo VanVoorhis
Noted lawyer of Fishers

Menzo's Prize Rooster

Menzo "By-the-Way" Van Voorhis, a prominent Rochester attorney, lived at the corner of Main Street, Fishers and Log Cabin Road and was very fond of raising fancy breeds of chickens. One day a hobo got off a freight train and asked for food at the Van Voorhis door. It was given to him.

The hobo, who himself had chickens (or so he stated) of a very fine quality back in the west, became an instant friend. Conversation centered around a very fine rooster strutting about in the yard. Menzo said, "By the way, I would give $30 for a rooster just like him." The hobo paused for a moment and said that he knew just where he could get one.

The next morning he returned with a rooster in a bag and collected the cash. According to Menzo, he got what he asked for—his own rooster.

Blue Ribbons vs Red

When the temperance movement got off to a good start in the 1870s, the Fishers and Valentown lodges put on plays, such as *Ten Nights in a Barroom* and *Muskegan Nigger*. They signed the famous Father Francis Murphy pledge, which read,

> "To abstain from all intoxicating liquors as a beverage and that I will by all honorable means, encourage others to abstain."

Each signer wore a blue ribbon. In the spirit of fun, the patrons of the Fishers Hotel saloon wore red ribbons. They challenged each other to ball games and other bits of rivalry.

One day the Red Ribbon Boys challenged their rivals to a match of human strength. The date was set for Saturday, July 4, 1903. The place was to be on the lawn in the rear of the hotel next to the livery stable. From the end of the stable to everybody's "Uncle" Johnny Hailey's barn was a high board fence plastered with circus posters to be seen from the passenger trains. It was like a field-day festival setting. Some of the boys who were non-members slept all night on the inside platform of the railroad water tower. Before daybreak they began shooting the cannon to announce the glorious fourth. Charles Wiley had forged some two inch high rectangular rings to fit the top of the anvils. The rings were then filled with gunpowder brought from the nearby Rand Powder Mills. Other anvils were then placed over the powder filled rings and long fuses were attached. When they were

Kingsley "King" Brownell

shot off, the explosions were deafening. Gregory Hill told me that he and others placed the anvils too close to the railroad station and when the detonation came, it blasted out all of the windows on that side of the station. Through some unknown cause, a keg of powder blew up in Perry Flynn's face. He was badly burned, but did not lose his eyesight.

The various events for the tests of strength began after dinner next door to King Brownell's saw mill. Timbers of increasing sizes were lifted and carried. Ernest Barry lifted a heavy pitch-laden railroad tie and carried it a mile. No one else cared to duplicate the feat. King, one of the blue-ribbon boys, was a veteran of the Civil War who had a part of his side shot away by a cannon ball during a cavalry charge. Always with a good-sized notch in his side, he recovered very well and was back to his pre-war hobby of demonstrating acts of strength. One act was rolling a 450 pound barrel of water up on his chest over his head and off his back. King Brownell has been called the "Samson of the

Genesee" for his many unusual exhibitions of strength.

More fun than the demonstrations of strength was the event of the greased pig. William F. Fisher donated a well-greased pig to be awarded to the person who could catch and hang onto it. No one could do it! It was driven back home.

The shotput, or throwing a ten-pound cannon ball the farthest, had more takers, but it came out a tie between my father, Almon P. Fisher, and Billy Flynn, both of whom were star baseball pitchers.

The next event was to see who could whirl the 200 pound anvil the farthest. A rope was attached around the anvil to get it off the ground and have something to hold onto for the swing. The first man up in line was Old Tom Morrisey. He took the rope in his teeth and whirled the anvil around with such velocity that when it was released it accidently demolished an outhouse with a man in it. Coupled with the loss of the railroad station's windows, Perry Flynn's accident, and the demolition of the necessary privy, the rest of the Fourth of July's features were cancelled.

Fisher's Railroad Station

Mrs. Woodin's Strange Death

A great deal of attention was focused upon Fishers in 1851, during a murder trial held in Canandaigua. Henry Woodin of Fisher Road was accused of murdering his second wife and throwing her body into the well outside.

Henry's first wife, Lydia, had died May 14, 1843, at the age of 45 and was buried in the Bushnell's Basin Cemetery. In the fall of 1843, Henry Woodin married Elizabeth A.; she had been married before and owned quite a bit of property. On August 17, 1844, the two were seen sitting at the opposite sides of a table in their home quarreling. The next morning her body was found floating in the well.

Henry packed his trunk and left for Plymouth, Michigan, a few miles west of Detroit. In a letter to Charles Fisher dated December 28, 1848, he wrote a full three page letter on all of the news out there. Excerpts of the letter give a little insight on his thinking: "It was with deep feeling of respect that I received your letter. It brought to mind the many happy days that I have enjoyed with you and your very kind family. In Plymouth Village we have both a Methodist and Presbyterian preaching. I have identified myself with them. Pray for me that I may acquit myself as one that must give an account at the judgment seat of Christ. There is the most profane language you ever heard. It makes me shudder to hear the men, women and children take such oaths. I have thrown in with the village lyceum. Our next debate—

Resolved: that profane swearing is the greatest evil in our Republic. I expect to have business east in the spring. If Mary Ann [his daughter] wants money for the children, please hand it to her and pay my taxes. I am not at all discouraged with my lot. Will not the judge of all the earth do right. My first purpose is to faithfully discharge the obligation that was entrusted to me to take care of my motherless children. There has just been a murder committed in Pontiac. A woman was the cause, I think. I shan't fight if all the women was to be killed in Michigan. Henry Woodin."

On a business trip back to Fishers from Michigan, Henry Woodin was arrested for the murder of his wife. The trial started on January 19, 1851, and lasted until January 24th. The District Attorneys, S. V. R. Mallory and Mr. Chatfield, had little evidence other than that Mrs. Woodin was found in the well and from the appearance that only one person had slept in the bed. The question was: was it murder or suicide? The formidable group of defense lawyers were Alvah Worden, Jacob P. Faurot, and Elbridge G. Lapham, later a U.S. Congressman and Senator. The jury could not agree, and the case was never tried again. Twenty-nine local witnesses were called at the trial, friends and neighbors of Henry Woodin. Judge William F. Allen of Oswego presided with County Judge Charles J. Folger, and Justices Swift and Smith formed the court.

On January 4, 1853, Henry Woodin deeded his farm to Henry Van Voorhis.

Henry Woodin headed a group of Fishers people who settled in Isabella County, Michigan. Henry Junior built a saw and grist mill on the Chippewa River and owned 1,050 acres which he farmed. His father is said to have fallen across a saw and was cut in two.

Henry Woodin Junior's wife was Sarah Barber Rose, one of

seven children of William and Anna Barber Rose who lived in the log cabin on Log Cabin Road. The Barber home was later the Battams' house on Fisher Road, now the property of the John Moffat family; the Barber graves are still near the driveway. Sarah's two brothers, Washington and Norman, were prominent in the Fishers community life. Norman served in the 102nd New York Infantry with Martin V. B. Snyder and other local boys during the Civil War. Norman sold his Fishers mill and went to work in Henry Woodin's mill in Michigan, where he was killed in 1878. Norman's descendants still live there.

In the Bushnell's Basin Cemetery is another Woodin, the father of Henry Senior. He was Amos Woodin, who died in Fishers on October 19, 1842, at the age of 89. He was a distinguished soldier and saw General Burgoyne surrender at Saratoga in 1777.

Strange things have happened through the years at the Woodin house. The apparitions are always of a woman or of a man and woman wrestling. Passersby have noticed peculiar lights around the outside well. The figure of a woman would go through the wall where there was once a door. Children have had trouble sleeping because of seeing the woman and would have their parents sit up with them until finally falling asleep. Through the years I have quizzed the various residents who have lived in the house. Many others have never seen or heard a thing.

Margaret Van Voorhis Smith, who was born and brought up in the Woodin house, told me that her family learned to live with this situation. What got her, she said, was when an elderly lady once called at the house about 1890 and asked for a drink of water out of the old well. The woman then said, "I suppose you wonder why I asked for a drink from this well. It was where my mother was killed."

Henry Garling's Mad Cow

About the year 1920, Henry Garling's docile cow went mad. It was being pastured in our field at the corner of Main Street, Fishers and Fisher Road. The son, William, came to lead it home one night to be milked. The cow refused to go. William pulled and I pushed, but to no avail. The cow broke loose and staggered to a small depression in the ground where some liquid was oozing out, and she began to drink it. The cow still refused to leave.

William Garling lost his temper and began beating the cow. The cow charged him and chased him up a cherry tree and began frothing at the mouth. We got a rope on its halter and snubbed it to the tree. William went home and got a gun and shot the cow, because there had been a rabies scare in the neighborhood. The cow was decapitated and the remainder buried on the spot. The head was boxed and sent to Cornell University for a rabies test. The report was negative, but the blood showed an alcohol content. No one could figure out where the alcohol came from, and so it was forgotten.

Strange things kept happening at these corners. Dogs and animals acted as if they were sick. Pheasants tried to fly but could not. Skunks and woodchucks were slow in getting out of the way of cars and were killed.

One day I found the answer while going over some family records. In the 1820s there had been a distillery on the creek at these corners. It was operated by Samuel Chandler and John Woolston. A great deal of corn was raised on the freshly cleared soil, but poor transportation to the outside world fostered a glutted local market. By turning the corn into whiskey there was a ready sale at 18¢ a gallon. In order to make it safe for drinking, the whiskey had to go through an aging process which could take years. The water power of Irondequoit Creek operated a device which held barrels so that they were steadily rocked day and night to speed the aging. Deals were also made with boatmen on Lake Ontario to place barrels of whiskey as ballast on the ships so as to take advantage of the rocking by the waves. After this the barrels of whiskey had to be kept at an even temperature in underground vaults or buried in the ground for a definite period.

In the late 1820s and early 1830s the temperance movement and religious revivals had a strong influence; the Fishers distillery went out of business. Nobody bothered to dig up the whiskey in the treated oak barrels. Once in awhile a heavy farm machine would collapse a weakened barrel. The whiskey was then exposed to the surface, intoxicating those who chose to drink it. Some self-appointed experts estimate that during the past 150 years this whiskey could now be aged to almost pure alcohol.

* * *

About the year 1818 Philip Bonesteele came here and bought the old Rowley Tavern on the site of the present Turk Hill Road entrance to Eastview Mall. He renamed it the "Popular Tavern" and bought his whiskey from Chandler & Woolston who bottled in fancy flasks. These flasks, now collectors items, bring high prices. Mr. Bonesteele "got religion," joined the temperance movement and closed his tavern to concentrate on farming. He constructed the present cobblestone mansion. His grandson,

Frank, hauled a load of these old flasks and tavern rubbish and dumped them into a ravine which is now the site of Sibley's store.

The Bonesteeles' tavern got rough at times with too much drinking. The biggest trouble maker was a man by the name of Bob Elton, who owned considerable property and was obnoxious in the way in which he obtained it. There was only one man who was able to deter Elton, and he was John Lane.

The Elton-Lane feud started when Lane bought his farm on Daily Road. Lane had raised some good cattle and Elton wanted to buy them at his own price, but Lane refused to sell. Thereupon Elton struck Lane over the face with a whip and for that Elton received a good beating.

John Lane was a veteran of the American Revolution and always wore a tricorn hat, and in cool weather he wore a flowing cape. On a late afternoon Elton had been demanding free drinks. When he didn't get them he started to tear the place apart. He attacked John Lane with a chair and then ran for his horse with Lane right after him on his horse. Down the Lower Fishers Road they raced until they got to Judge Fisher's house where Elton demanded protection. Instead, Elton was placed on a peace bond. The feud was so much discussed that when at twilight the sounds of heavy hoofbeats are heard on the Lower Fishers Road or thunder is heard in the distance some believe it is Elton and Lane still feuding.

The Courtship of Helen Jane

A 54 year-old father found himself contesting with his 16 year-old son for the hand of a 30 year-old girl in the 1840s. The father was Charles Fisher, whose lumber mill, flour mill and 1,000 acres of land had made him a leading citizen in the region surrounding the Fishers Station on the Auburn and Rochester Raiload. The son, Robert, was one of five children by Charles Fisher and his wife, Rebecca Gaskill Fisher, who had died two years earlier. The girl was the attractive Helen Jane Pardee, graduate of Genesee Wesleyan Seminary in nearby Lima. She was accomplished in music, student of the classics and a daughter of Henry Pardee, member of the New York State Assembly for several years and a prominent figure in Ontario County.

Robert was at a distinct disadvantage. While admired by Helen Jane for his quick wit, intelligence and interest in the law, he was young, lacked advanced education and was not yet self-supporting. His father proposed that if Robert would give up his thoughts of Helen Jane, he would send Robert to the new University of Rochester, for which Charles Fisher had given money and helped raise funds. Robert reluctantly agreed to end his pursuit, on those terms. Later he left to join his older brother, Charles, Jr., in the practice of law in Bement, Illinois.

With Robert out of the picture, Charles Fisher, with his considerable resources, moved to make his home more fitting for a person of Helen Jane Pardee's tastes and background. He added

Helen Jane Pardee Fisher

On her wedding day, October 21, 1850, Fishers, New York.
Ninety mink were trapped by the groom, Charles Fisher, to make
the fur wedding coat.

to the 1811 family homestead, a Greek Revival style front wing with formal parlor. He purchased a fine black glass-windowed coach, showpiece of the community, which could be drawn by two or four of his black horses. For it he built a carriage house with male servant quarters upstairs.

Helen Jane liked Charles Fisher, whom she affectionately called "the Squire." She also liked what she saw. They were married on a Monday noon, October 21, 1850, an unseasonable warm day, in the old First Baptist Church in nearby Mendon by the Reverend W. F. Parrish. After the ceremony, the new coach, with the newlyweds, led a procession back to the Fisher homestead for a sumptuous luncheon on the lawn. Music was provided under the trees by stringed instrument players from Genesee Wesleyan. Among the wedding presents was a full-length coat Charles had made for his bride from 90 minks he had trapped in his Tamarack Swamp.

Within a few years, Helen Jane Pardee Fisher found herself in charge of a rather extended household. She and her husband had two sons, Henry Pardee Fisher, born in 1851, and William Frank Fisher, born three years later. In 1854 her aging father, Henry Pardee, sold his farm on Pardee (now Plaster Mill) Road near Victor and then with three daughters, Helen Jane's own sister, Ann, and two half-sisters, Alice and Amelia with her husband, William Blackmon, moved in with Helen Jane. Also moving in for a time were Henry's stepdaughter, Mary, and her brother, Ezra Wilmarth, who later successfully searched for gold in the Rocky Mountains, California and Australia. Other young family members were nephew Charles Fisher Curtis and granddaughter Harriet Day, whose mother, Harriet Fisher Day, had died soon after childbirth in 1847.

Managing the more menial household details with help of several other servants was Margaret Robinson, 30, newly arrived from Scotland. Adding more international flavor to the rural scene was the Polish carriage boy, Timothy Rishman, 18, who was succeeded by Tyler Squires in 1855. Helen Jane was free to look after the needs of the families of relatives, workmen and tenant farmers living in the seventeen homes and five farms 'Squire' Fisher owned in the surrounding area among them one in Mendon and another in Perinton on Aldrich Road.

All was not duty for Helen Jane. Fisher's Station, now simply Fishers, was only 15 miles from the thriving city of Rochester, and the newlyweds had a suitable coach to take them over the plank roads to social events in the city. When Jenny Lind, the "Swedish Nightingale," sang at Corinthian Hall in Rochester on July 24, 1851, Helen Jane and the Squire were there. They were at Corinthian Hall again on November 13 of the next year when Ole Bull, the Norwegian violin virtuoso, brought Adelina Patti to Rochester. There were also the gala balls of the New York State Militia, of which Charles Fisher had been an officer for more than 40 years.

The families of both the Squire and Helen Jane were involved with historic events. Squire's Grandfather, John Fisher, a sea captain, happened to be home the night of the Boston Tea Party on December 16, 1773, and participated. When he got home his boots were full of tea, and so he and his wife, Mary, went up in the attic and steeped tea away from prying eyes. Charles and Helen Jane's first family party was a re-enactment of that attic tea party, using the same teapot and cups and saucers on the 77th anniversary, December 16, 1850. This writer repeated that family party on the 200th anniversary.

Helen Jane was the hostess for a New York State Militia Ball in her home on April 30, 1854, to commemorate the 65th anniversary of President George Washington's inauguration in New York City in 1789. Helen Jane's grandfather, Silas Pardee, a

Fisher Homstead—1927
Built in 1811 and enlarged in 1849. At one time in the
mid-1850s it served as home for 23 family members.

Revolutionary War veteran who came to Victor in 1807, had attended the inauguration. Henry Pardee wore his father's coat with the famous inaugural buttons made especially for the occasion.

During other hours Helen Jane developed her skills of making hats and dresses. Her father died in 1862 at the Fisher homestead and 10 years later, at the age of 74, the Squire was laid to rest in the family cemetery across the street.

Out in Illinois, Robert Fisher had established a successful career as an attorney, among his clients was the Wabash Railroad. He had married a widow, Lucinda Ellis, who had two children of her own. Lucinda died in 1872, nine days after Charles Fisher. Back to Fishers came Robert; again he was rejected by Helen Jane. Robert, however, remained in Ontario County and stayed after Helen Jane's death in 1893. He practiced law and served as a highly respected justice for the Town of Victor until his death in the Fisher homestead in 1914, at the age of 80.

During his last years in the homestead he was surrounded by growing grandchildren of his father and Helen Jane's son, William. Robert Fisher's favorite great-niece, upon whom he lavished much attention and taught to talk, was named Helen Fisher.

Treasure Troves

Mrs. X.

Mrs. X. was a very frugal old lady. Her husband worked hard all of his life and had banked every possible bit of his earnings. The living necessities were raised on the farm, and agricultural tools were purchased at bargain prices at auctions. When an opportunity came along to buy an adjoining farm, he bought it. The hard work of farming finally took its toll, and Mr. X. died.

Mrs. had some difficulties with her husband's bank account so she withdrew the $40,000 and closed the account. This, it is known, was not placed in any bank. Her friends tried to give her advice, which only drove her to a more secluded life. She sold the adjoining farm for $24,000, as was recorded by the deed tax. This money also was never deposited in a bank.

An elderly neighbor of Mrs. X. who wanted to help her was rudely rebuffed like everyone else. He started watching her with binoculars. He was surprised one day to see her take fruit cans outside of her house and bury them in her backyard. Shortly after this she died.

The new owners practically pulled the house apart trying, to no avail, to find the money. My old friend was deeply puzzled as to what to do and to whom he should report what he knew. He came to me for advice. We discussed the situation at some length.

We reasoned that since the new owner was noted for his lack of generosity, my friend could expect no reward of any kind if he revealed the information. Therefore, we agreed that he was to keep quiet until an opportunity came along so that he could buy the property and retrieve the treasure.

Before my friend died, he pointed out to me the site of the buried treasure. In the years since there has been no change in the property purchase possibilities, and besides, the people keep dogs. What to do? What to do?

Alvin Parks

About 1926 a stranger called at the home of my cousin, Irma Reed Locke, at the east end of Main Street, Fishers. He said that he was from Rochester and had never been out this way before, but had seen her house and farm in a dream some time ago. For months he had traveled over many roads seeking the location of his dream, and now he had found it.

He had a proposition he wanted to make, which amused her very much. In the dream he had seen a man burying a large box of money and other valuables. The stranger wanted permission to dig for the treasure in her presence, and he would split the find with her if she would allow him to do so. Mrs. Locke said that she thought that the whole idea was very foolish, but to humor him she agreed to let him dig. The site the man wanted to dig was along a hedgerow on the northern part of the farm, just west of the grading for the New York Thruway. The exact spot is now under the eastbound lane at the new Benson Road intersection.

The man had been digging for an hour when Mrs. Locke and her husband, Louis, arrived. He was beginning to scrape dirt away from a rusted metal box he had just exposed. Mrs. Locke told me she was astounded that such a box was on her property. Mr. Locke went for a jimmy bar while the box was being hauled to the surface.

When the box was opened, it contained a mass of silver dollars and gold coins, along with several pairs of silver candlesticks. All of this was evenly divided on the spot. Mrs. Locke got quite worried that this loot might be the work of robbers who had stashed it away and were never able to take it back. She got the treasure hunter to agree to give it up if it was found to have been stolen. That problem was solved when it was found that the coins were all dated before 1856.

Mrs. Locke sold me a pair of the Russian silver candlesticks, which I sold to Mrs. Ruth Webb Lee, who later became the leading authority on early glass through her books on the subject. Mrs. Locke's share of the old coins were sold at auction, which financed her husband's inventions and an investment in the Stever-Locke Company factory in Honeoye Falls.

It was eventually concluded that the money belonged to Alvin Parks, an early owner of the farm who died in 1856. He was a commodity merchant and carried large sums of money in his travels between the east and the west. He always had two armed guards who were local boys, whom he could trust. Alvin was Irma Locke's grandfather, and she used to tell me many tales of his buying and selling trips to the midwest and of his financial dealings in New York City. She said that he was always so relieved when he got off the train at Fishers to be free of the tension of being robbed. As there were no local banks which were really safe in the days before the Civil War.

Alvin Parks married my great-aunt Susan Freeman. The succeeding generations have been close to us. My grandmother, Addie Preston Fisher, a niece of Susan's, spent her summers with her studying piano under her daughter, Alice Parks. One day, following a heavy cloudburst, my grandmother was on her way home to the Fisher homestead from Valentown Hall when an accident happened. As she was driving down the hill where the treasure was found, the roaring water through the sluiceway frightened the horse and tipped the buggy over into the stream. My father, who was a baby in a long dress, was swept downstream. Just as he was being sucked into the sluice, Reece Reed pulled him out and revived him. This accident was a close call for me, as well as for my brothers and sisters!

Mr. A.

Mr. A. was a good friend of mine and did not have faith in banks. He never told his wife where he kept his money, nor was she much concerned to know. One day he had a stroke and couldn't talk and was taken to the hospital. Before he died, he revived for a time and tried very hard to tell his wife where he had hidden some $12,000 in cash. She sought my help in trying to interpret his last words, which sounded like either picture or pitcher. I couldn't help. He might have hidden the money in a recess behind a picture or even in a water pitcher, but all meant nothing to Mrs. A.

Mrs. M.

One evening Mrs. M, a very delightful neighbor, invited my wife and me over to her house. She seemed a little nervous and after a period of friendly conversation, announced that she at last had a chance to buy back into her family a large mahogany secretary, a treasured heirloom which she had longed to own.

Years ago, when an ancestor's home was sold at auction, certain family jewels and important documents never came to light. She believed that they must have been hidden in some secret compartment of the secretary. Would I know how to find such a place?

I walked over to the secretary and ran my fingers along and under a slight ledge, pressed up into two holes, and out popped a wide drawer full of just the things that she was looking for. Mrs. M. just sat there speechless and motionless, waiting for us to leave, which we did.

Benson Gold

The discovery of gold in the west helped the father of two local boys to build two fine brick houses on Benson Road, as the result of his panning operations in California. James and Alonzo built up three good farms of which a part of one is still in the family.

Wilmarth

Ezra Wilmarth, grandson of Ezra Wilmarth, who built the Wilmarth Tavern on Boughton Hill, was a Fishers school teacher who headed for the gold fields of California in April, 1858. Arriving in New York City, he found all ships overbooked. In a letter to his stepfather, Henry Pardee, my great-grandfather, he wrote that he took passage to the gold mines of Australia, where he spent nine years. From there he went to California, Nevada and Montana. He sailed back home from San Francisco via the Isthmus of Panama.

In November, 1867, he arrived back in Fishers. The Fisher family didn't know him at first, because of his full beard. He emptied a large belt full of gold dust and nuggets on the kitchem table. Our family has kept some of these nuggets as souvenirs. He had other types of gifts for each member of the family. For his half-sister, Alice Pardee, he brought the first green parrot to be seen in this county. He caught it while walking across the Isthmus of Panama. For his other half-sister, Helen Pardee Fisher, he brought a beautiful shell basket, which he bought in Acapulco, Mexico.

The quiet life of Fishers was more than Ezra Wilmarth could stand, for the lure of gold and adventure was always tugging at him. Before starting on his next trip, with Ben Collins of Bushnell's Basin, he went to Coldwater, Michigan, to bid goodbye to his sister, Mrs. Mary Wilmarth Daniels, who had been brought up in the Fisher household.

According to his diary, on the 15th day of April, 1868, they left his sister's home for the headwaters of the Missouri River above Fort Benton and then went into the Rocky Mountain gold region. After an absence of many months, he returned and stocked the Fisher family coffers with more of his surplus gold. He left a supply of mementos of gold bags, photos, letters and his Army Colt .44 revolver. He then again headed for the gold fields in Australia, where he died in 1880.

His interesting story-form diary was also left at the Fisher homestead. His last entry was:

> The vicissitudes of life changed the character of almost all men, but in different manners; prosperity and adversity being the principal powers in affecting it. Yes, the romance (of our tour to the gold mines, as some would romantically express it) is at an end; and now the stern realities of life stare us resolutely in the face as if to bar our further progress; and strong and brave will be the heart that tramples down the barrier and returns (whether pecuniarily successful or otherwise) a contented man.
>
> Fond to the uninitiated, who may perchance, peruse these lines, whether young, middle-aged, or

old, let me say: do not let the magnified glitter of far distant mines, or any other of the curiosities of this world induce you to leave a now happy home; for if you do, MARK MY WORDS, you will regret it to the last day of your life.

I speak from an experience of ten years wandering around on the face of the globe; true, at times I have had my share of the good things of earth, and at times enjoyed myself to the full extent of the word; still, there was an aching void in my heart that refused to be satisfied; and could only be partially appeased when my mind wandered back to the scenes of my childhood, and rested on the imaginary forms of those long since left behind; for however false a man may be to the world, to his home he will ever prove true.

After an elapse of many years, I return, only to leave it again after a short sojourn—RESTLESS and DISCONTENTED. I may be an exception to the rest of mankind, and for their sake it is to be hoped I am; for life is short and for the success and enjoyment thereof,

All have the sincere wishes of

E. R. Wilmarth.

Preston-Reed

Benjamin Franklin Freeman of Orleans, Cape Cod, with his wife, Charlotte Wing of Brewster, Cape Cod, and children of Pilgrim descent, got off a canal packet boat at Bushnell's Basin and walked to Victor via Fishers. They lodged at Simeon Parks' place until their house was built in Victor. The entries in Charles Fisher's mill book, show he provided the lumber for the Freeman house in 1830.

In 1842 the Freeman family moved to Battle Creek, Michigan. In 1855 their daughter, Emaline, married Almon Ephraim Preston. He was a prominent furniture manufacturer and a member of the state assembly of Michigan. During the Civil War, as a captain, he raised a cavalry company known as the Merrill Horse. As an inventor, he held many patents and was the creator of a machine to make the first wire nails. He owned large tracts of land in Michigan and property in downtown Chicago.

Emaline and Almon's daughter, Adeline Preston, married William Fisher, September 6, 1882 in Michigan. Almon Preston then divided his time between Fishers and Michigan, helping to finance and make the Fisher farm into a magnificent showplace as a nursery and produce sales property.

Susan Freeman (sister to Emaline Freeman Preston) Parks' daughter, Charlotte, married Reece Reed, and they lived in the Parks homestead. Thereupon her wealthy uncle, Almon E. Preston, made Reece Reed a working partner in a gold mining project in Colorado. The Reed family then lived part of the time in Denver and part of the time at the Parks homestead in Fishers. The gold was processed and banked in Chicago, where the profits were divided.

Reece Reed had to transport his share of the money home by rail. Finally the secret of the money got out, and he was followed on one of his last trips home. His wife, Charlotte "Lottie" Parks Reed, met him at the station for the late train. Two strange men also got off and watched while the baggageman helped load the box of money into the buckboard wagon. As they raced away up Main Street towards home, shots were fired as the men on foot tried to catch them. It was very dark and stormy, and about halfway home Reece stopped and dumped the money down a woodchuck hole, covered it over, and replaced the contents of the box with stones.

The strangers caught him at his home and stole the box and hurried away. Shortly after that the maid poisoned Mr. and Mrs.

Reed by putting arsenic in the food. Neighbors driving by saw them out on the lawn, rolling in agony. They survived the poisoning, but it left Reece Reed a very sick man. It was suspected that the robbers were in league with the maid, for while they were sick, the house was ransacked for the money, which they did not find. Their daughter, Irma Reed Locke, never did know where her father kept the money, but she believed that he had a secret compartment built into the house. Someday, when remodeling is done, it will be exposed. Such an event happened a few years ago in the house of Willis Hill on Willis Hill Road, when a secret closet was exposed by carpenters remodeling that house.

Charles "Squire" Fisher

Squire Fisher's Open House

Squire Fisher's house was always open to travelers and was a gathering place for civic enterprises, some national in scope. When Charles "Squire" Fisher came with his parents in 1811, from his birthplace in Stockbridge, Massachusetts, they built a log cabin. In a few years he bought a sawmill so he could make a frame addition to the log cabin. In 1849 part of the original cabin was replaced with a two-story Greek Revival wing. An opposite east wing had already been added to house the Fishers post office. At one time fifteen family members and seven servants lived in the house.

The saw mill prospered as other new houses were being built but still a surplus of lumber piled up with no market because of the lack of a year-round shipping facility. The Erie Canal, opened in 1825, made only summer shipments to eastern markets. Because experiments were being made in the east with steam railroads, a meeting was held at the homestead in 1827 to consider a railroad through the Finger Lakes country from Rochester to Syracuse. The idea met with approval, and ten years later the railroad was actually started. The family doctor, Dr. Hartwell Carver of Pittsford, attended and also proposed a transcontinental railroad. Dr. Carver pursued his idea until its completion in 1869 at Promontory Point, Utah.

The Fisher family joined the Mendon Baptist Church. Other members at that time were Brigham Young, a furniture maker;

Hartwell Carver, MD

He became famous as the "Father of the Transcontinental Railroad and promoted it through Congress until it was completed in 1869. He was the family doctor for many residents of the Fishers area.

Heber C. Kimball, a potter; and the Tomlinson and Parks families. Brigham Young was hired to put window panes in the Fisher homestead and to build a house next door. Baptist socials and meetings were held at the Fisher home. In the winter of 1832 five Mormon missionaries came to Mendon, holding meetings in homes including some in the large dining room of the Fisher's. There were so many Mormon converts that it amounted to a raid on the Mendon Baptist Church. The Mormon converts later moved to Kirtland, Ohio.

In 1847, Spiritualism was started by the Fox sisters. The Squire's daughter, Almira, died in 1847, and the next year his wife, Rebecca, died. In his grief he took up Spiritualism and held "Light" meetings at his home, which became an outpost for that religion with visits by the Fox sisters and other leaders. Sister Margretta Fox left her tortoise-shell hair comb there by mistake.

The Baptist Church in the Rochester area wanted a college, and in 1847 proposed to move Colgate University to this city. The leading promoters instead decided to establish a new university, the University of Rochester. Receipts to Charles Fisher from the new university show that he provided a substantial sum of money. The fund-raising trustees were overnight guests of the Squire during their campaign in the Town of Mendon.

When the Fishers Hotel overflowed with customers, the Squire always found room at his house. On their way to settle on western land in the fall of 1852, Henry Van Voorhis and his family got off the train at Fishers. The Squire put them up for the night. Because they liked the local hospitality, they bought a farm upon which their descendants still live.

About 1831 the Canandaigua Academy debating team competed with a Fishers team and spent the night at the Squire's house. Stephen A. Douglas was on the Canandaigua team and left two years later to seek his fortune in Illinois. During his presidential campaign against Lincoln he came back to see his mother and sister in Clifton Springs and gave a memorable speech in the park. On his way back over the Auburn Road he stopped in Fishers to greet old friends and seek votes.

Dr. Charles Came of Pittsford presented his famous "Scientific Exhibition" in 1840 in the Fishers schoolhouse and spent the night at the Squire's house. For over fifty years this show was hauled in a covered wagon from Maine to Michigan. This extensive collection is now one of the main features at the Valentown Museum.

Another stopover guest at the Squire's house was Susan B. Anthony, who was seeking public support for her upcoming Canandaigua trial for voting illegally in the presidential election of 1872. The Squire's widow, Helen Jane Fisher, said in a letter to her sister that "Susan talked good sense."

Although Squire Fisher died in 1872, his son, William Fisher, was for a number of years host to John Burroughs, the great naturalist and author, who was botanizing in the area with his party.

The planners for a Fishers Fire Department met there in 1916, but their plan was set aside in favor of organizing the Fishers Home Defense Reserve, Company F for 1917–19, a part of the Ontario County Battalion with my father, Captain Almon Preston Fisher, as the commander and using the homestead as the official headquarters. This writer is the sole surviving member of the seventy men who served in Company F.

The years 1930, 1931, and 1932 were busy years at the homestead when several hundred people attended the Fishers School reunions on the spacious front lawn.

In 1933 the lawn was the setting for a "Pioneer Day"

pageant to depict the history of Fishers, written and directed by this author. One hundred and fifty people were in the cast.

I also wrote and directed a pageant, presented on June 30, 1953, showing Dr. Hartwell Carver's part in projecting the Transcontinental Railroad. A few of the vice-presidents of the railroads even got involved by playing some of the characters in the pagent.

Five generations have used Squire Fisher's house as a center for community activities.

The 1922 home built Fishers Fire Truck
driven by US Senator Kenneth B. Keating.

A Trip to Venice

An elaborate wedding and a social whirl of twenty years and a long planned trip to Venice ended with only a gift of a large painting of a scene in that famous city on the Adriatic Sea.

When Helen Jane Pardee married "Squire" Charles Fisher on October 21, 1850, one of his gifts to his bride was to be a trip to Venice. Increased business activities in his mills and farms in Fishers kept delaying their anticipated trip to Europe. After the Civil War, the Squire, who was twenty-two years older than Jane, was advised not to take such a strenuous trip.

One day in 1871 a man by the name of F. Perken got off the train at Fishers and went to the Squire's office and asked for a job. One of his numerous qualifications was having been an artist in Boston and New York. He was asked if he would be willing, for the price of a round trip by steamer for two to Europe, to paint a scene of Venice for the Squire's home. He agreed and said that he would have it finished within a year. The painting was to be eight feet high and twelve feet wide so as to fit the whole end of a room and be stored on a roller.

Space was cleared in Fishers Hall upstairs over Asa Wiley's blacksmith shop. Artist Perken was given an English Staffordshire dish with a transfer picture of a scene in Venice, possibly from a famous painting by Titian of the Grand Canal. In the foreground are elegantly garbed ladies and gentlemen by a marble balustraded garden who were about to take a gondola ride. In the background is the church of Santa Maria della Salute, which dates from the 1600s.

According to my friend George Hill, who was a boy at the time, the project stimulated much local interest in the field of art. Some outstanding artists who came to view the work were: portrait artist John Parks, landscape painter Eleanor Parks, and Alice Parks who had painted the gilded china dinner set for the Vanderbilt-Whitney wedding in New York City. Certain times were set aside during the day for the public to see the progress of the much talked-about painting.

The painting was done within the specified time for hanging. The Squire was very sick and the painting was hung in the parlor where he lay on an antique daybed just before he died on that same day, May 4, 1872. After all the intervening years, Helen Jane and Charles finally did see Venice together through this beautiful painting.

For the next fifty years the painting was borrowed as a backdrop for plays and stage settings around the community and especially on the stage of Valentown Hall. After years of storage in the Fisher family attic, it was given to the Valentown Museum.

The Great Ball of Fire

An important event, which never received newspaper recognition, happened one night in the year 1894. A visitor from outer space came roaring through the sky, and with an earth-shaking crash, buried itself into a knoll on Fisher Road.

Miss Miranda Woolston, who lived below the hill in the old Woolston Homestead on Railroad Mills Road, often would point out the spot where the visitor landed. Miranda said, "During the early evening a roar like a violent storm coming up, shook the house and frightened everyone." No one in the family could figure out what had happened, but they knew something hit the ground. The next morning's search of the farm by her father, Franklin Woolston, revealed a big hole in the upper field on Fisher Road.

The hole was about fifteen feet across and thirty feet deep with dirt thrown up in all directions. Mr. Woolston realized that this hole was not caused by any ordinary sinking of the ground. He got word to the University of Rochester geologist, Professor Herman LeRoy Fairchild, who came out the next day on the Auburn Road train to the Railroad Mills station and was taken by horse and buggy up the hill to the hole.

An extension ladder was so placed that the professor could explore the cavity. Men helped dig further down, but no solid mass could be found as far as they dug. It was believed to have been a meteorite which went deeper into the ground or exploded and vaporized upon impact. Mr. Woolston took a wagon load of rock samples to the University. It took years to fill the crater with rubbish and field rakings, Miranda said.

I talked to the late George W. Hill, who said that he saw the flash of the meteorite in the sky that night. He was standing outside of his house on the Mendon Road scanning the sky, for he said that he seemed to expect that something was going to happen. Then it did happen. His neighbors also rushed out of their houses to see what had happened but by the time they got out, nothing could be seen. The next morning he crossed the Fishers valley to see if he could find where the fireball landed and found the people who were looking into the hole in the ground.

He tramped down the hill to Crossman's Pond and noticed that the normally-clear pond was all muddy. Since his youth George had always taken an interest in the pond, and every few years he would take a depth measurement. It had long been known, even in late years, as a bottomless pond. In 1890 George found it to be 210 feet deep. On this day in 1894 it had filled in some 60 feet. He questioned others with his thought that the meteor impact might have had some connection with the muddy pond.

My friend, Frank Pugsley of Pittsford, in 1894 was employed by Professor Henry A. Ward in his famous Ward's Natural Science Museum in Rochester. His job was sawing off slabs of siderites and aerolites for sale. Professor Ward was then in the process of building up the world's largest collection of meteorites. Ward and Pugsley took their turn at digging for the meteorite. They gave up, for they did not have sounding instruments nor power excavators.

This information came to light when, years ago, I asked Mr. Pugsley if he knew anything about the meteorite. On that night while he was walking home in Pittsford he heard a hissing roar pass overhead like a big ball of fire. Since he recognized what it was, it didn't scare him like it did his neighbors. As a token for my interest, he gave me a small slab of a siderite, which he had sawed off while at Ward's.

An interesting aftermath to the crater hole came the following year, 1895. Miss Miranda Woolston with Harvey Southgate and other children were walking along the high cliff above Irondequoit Creek and came upon a cave opening. She told her father, Franklin, about it and he remembered that his father, William, knew about it and had taken out a cache of flintlock muskets, pistols and some swords. These Miranda remembered as having been kept in a room in their barn until some person stole them. Her grandfather had capped over the cave because it was dangerous. Before the cave was capped over this time, my father took out some stalactites, which I still have, and a few years ago I removed more. Those who explored the cave in 1895 found that a tunnel went towards the meteorite hole. They assumed that the tunnel continued on under Crossman's Pond.

At the base of the hill next to the race track on West Main Street, Fishers, is a capstone between the clay and gray sand. This is the same material of which the cave roof is made. The stalactites and stalagmites are the supporting pillars of the cave. George Hill advanced the idea that when the meteorite struck the ground it broke through this cave tunnel and the great heat and pressure blew out the cave cap and at the same time affected the depth of Crossman's Pond.

My son, Douglas, and I had planned, when the situation was right, to get permission and then use modern methods to retrieve what Mr. Hill and Mr. Pugsley called the "Fishers Meteorite" but now a house has been built over the spot. For the sake of the owners, I just hope that the ground underneath will remain stable.

The Happy Well Digger

Hicks Artlip was known as the happiest man in town. He sang from sunup to sundown. He sometimes sang old favorites but mostly what he had made up. The only time that he didn't sing was when he ate and slept. Everybody loved to hear him sing, because of his melodious voice. He earned money at funerals, weddings and social gatherings and even singing square dance calls. No one could be angry in his presence long. If they couldn't sing with him, they would whistle his tune.

By trade Hicks Artlip was a well digger and a salesman for water pumps. His reputation as a dowser spread far and wide, because with his peach twig devining rod he was very successful in finding water. I remember him as a small old man, just the right size for getting down in a well to lay up the stones.

In 1892, the year that Grover Cleveland won the presidential election, Hicks Artlip sang this song:

"Oh, I'm a true American, in Fishers I do dwell. Like all true Americans I love my country well. Like all true Americans I love my country dear. For I'm a Cleveland Democrat and a Union Volunteer. Now shout boys shout and shout until the end. For the Democrats are on their taps and going to beat Ol' Ben [Harrison]. Now all of you Republicans, how sorry I feel for you. With your high tariff and Force Bill, you don't know what to do. But with Cleve and Steve [Adlai E. Stevenson] to lead us we have victory you know. For Dudley can't run the block of five as he did four years ago."

On pleasant evenings people would gather at the railroad station to have song fests. The local musicians were attracted and provided musical accompaniment. The Valentown Band composed of Fishers men gathered at the local bandstand and featured Hicks. In bad weather all would meet at the Valentown Hall ballroom and have dinner with a social afterwards. Some have claimed that barber shop singing really got its start here in 1880 in Seth Cole's barber shop at Valentown Hall. Seth's house still stands on West Main Street, Fishers.

Irish Wakes

The tradition of having a wake, a gathering of friends and relatives of the deceased, was a mark of respect. It helped the family with work and food, as well as creating an opportunity to say something nice about the departed. One of the jobs assumed by the friends was to prepare the body for the funeral and burial. These gatherings often got out of hand due to the copious flow of hard cider or just straight whiskey. Several accounts about these wakes have long lingered and been told at storytelling time.

A resident whose life had been a hardship to his family had fallen off a moving freight train while he was drunk and was killed. All of the family friends and neighbors gathered for the wake. Much time was spent with everybody just sitting around and saying nothing. Finally one man spoke up and said, "By golly, John was a good smoker," and then everyone departed for home.

Timothy "Right Turn" Welch died and his friends gathered for the wake. In the basement were several barrels of hard cider, which flowed freely for the guests. It came time to prepare the body for the funeral. The first thing they did was to get rid of a dirty growth of whiskers. The corpse was laid on the floor. One man held his head while another sat on his chest and worked away, hacking with a dull razor and not using shaving lather. All of the time the razor was getting duller and duller. Then all of a sudden the wake was thrown into a turmoil when another unsuccessful hack of the razor caused the corpse to sit up and ask what was going on. The old husband-and-wife feud was revived by the razor-pulling event, and Tim got a good broom beating for his alcoholic excesses.

Old man Baylor died and the usual flow of hard cider was constant at the wake. It was so constant that the corpse never did get prepared for the funeral. As the fermented apple juice knocked out the guests one by one, they were laid side by side next to the corpse on the floor. The next morning the undertaker came, took a body and placed it in a casket for the church service. The trip was made to the cemetery and the bearers lowered the remains into the ground. As the pastor intoned "ashes to ashes and dust to dust", a shovel full of stones and soil thundered down onto the casket making noise enough to wake the dead. A movement was noticed through the glass window. The intonations stopped and the mourners peered in the casket. As the top of the casket popped off, Mrs. Boyle shrieked, "That's my husband! That's not Mr. Baylor!"

Mr. Boyle was then raised from the dead, and Mr. Baylor was buried at the convenience of the family.

After Mr. Baylor's death a man by the name of McIntyre moved in and lived there until he died shortly after World War I. My father almost accidently killed Mr. McIntyre in 1914 when a shot from his army rifle missed a woodchuck on our hill, crossed the half mile valley, grazed his head, and lodged in the kitchen wall.

Mrs. Belinda Baylor was very conspicuous by always wearing long black Victorian dresses. The young folks referred to her as "old switchtail." In those days women did not smoke, but we noticed that Belinda reeked with tobacco smoke. We observed that when she went to the store, a small bag was always handed to her for which she made a payment. By watching closely we discovered that she was buying cigarettes. The youth of Fishers were shocked to find that the one who played the Sunday School piano was a smoking woman.

* * *

Mike O'Flarety was a brakeman on the Auburn Road, so he was gone for several days working as far as the East Syracuse yards. One day soon after he left home a brakeman was knocked off a moving freight train and killed when his head hit the protruding water spout at the Fishers station. None of the crew knew it or missed him, and the train moved on into the Rochester yards. The Fishers telegraph operator recognized the battered person as Mike O'Flarety. He had him taken over to his home at the Irish settlement known as Poverty Huddle. The relatives and neighbors were notified and the usual wake was held.

The home part of the funeral in the morning was all over, and the procession was about to leave when who should walk in but the real Mike O'Flarety. It is difficult to describe the chaos his arrival caused, first for Mike to stop his own funeral, and then for the O'Flaretys to find that they were not going to bury one of their own family but an unknown stranger.

Brady Brandy

"Parson" Brady had an insatiable desire to be rich. By working as a day laborer, he could just about make ends meet.

He was a good customer of the Fishers Hotel saloon. While there, he spent considerable time asking the patrons what type of drink they would like, other than what was available. "Parson" Brady studied the various fruits and wild herbs looking for ingredients to be used in a more pleasurable alcoholic drink. He tried out samples on his bar friends, discarding some and improving others of fermented wild berries and fruit juices, which made novel drinks. At last he developed a concoction, which he called Brady Brandy. His pals called for more and more of his drink so that he spent a considerable amount of time away from the saloon in order to produce the celebrated Brady Brandy.

He asked the local attorney, Menzo Van Voorhis, to get him a patent. While taking the necessary papers for the application to Mr. Van Voorhis, he was killed in his horse and buggy at the Fisher Road Crossing. The Auburn Road passenger train had just left the Fishers Station and was blowing its whistle approaching the next crossing. Flagman Charles Glass waved his warning sign, blew his whistle, and tried to block the horse and buggy— "Parson" Brady was too full of his success to stop.

The Fishers Road Crossing
Two photographers at left making a record where "Parson"
Brady was killed along with his horse.

The "Parson" was long remembered at the saloon by his much used quote: "What the hell is the use of being poor when a half pint will make you feel as rich as Vanderbilt? I don't drink it because I like it. I drink it for the effect of it."

The Ghost City of Valentown

Annual Community Festival and Antique Show
still draws customers to Valentown Hall

The Ghost City of Valentown

The Town and Valentine families aspired to build a village, hopefully a city, at the intersection of six roads a mile and a half from the Fishers railroad station.

Ichabod Town settled there in 1809 when these roads were still Indian trails. His log cabin was next to a cooper shop and a nearby blacksmith shop which he had built. In plowing the adjacent fields, he unearthed Indian trade axes. As Ichabod Town prospered, he built a Greek Revival house, at the intersection in 1830, but his hoped for village did not materialize because the area was composed of widely separated farm houses.

Town's daughter, Nancy, who inherited 140 acres of land, married Samuel Valentine. When the Civil War broke out in 1861, Samuel built a group of attached buildings for use as a store and barns. These he painted with red, white and blue stripes which caught the patriotic fancy of the Fishers people and began an annual 4th of July rally that lasted for 60 years. During war years exciting speeches and martial band music helped many young men to be recruited for the army.

In the 1870s, a survey line for a railroad was run from Pittsburgh to the port of Pulteneyville on Lake Ontario through the property now owned by Samuel's son, Levi Valentine. It was now Levi's turn to try to create a village. For the name of his project, he took his mother's family name, Town, and added it to part of his father's to make Valentown. To help the sale of his land for industrial and commercial purposes, he believed that he needed a "business block" to house as many establishments as possible. So up went an enormous, three-story frame building, 80 feet long and 35 feet wide, complete with a large attic and a basement having a stable for 80 horses with an above ground entrance.

Tenants were immediately found for specific uses. Nine doors opened along the front porch. A general store, meat market, harness shop, barber and cobbler shops, bakery and restaurant were on the ground floor. Four stairways to the upper floors gave access to a large room for farmers who belonged to the Grange, a school of acting, a music school, an art school and a school of business. The 18 foot high grand ballroom with four chandeliers occupied most of the third floor.

School of Acting

The building of Valentown Hall in 1879 stimulated the organization of many clubs. They all needed inexpensive entertainment. A retired theatre man was hired to establish a school to teach acting, elocution and singing. C. W. Richardson had conducted such a school in Oswego and in other cities. His reputation brought many students from surrounding towns and Rochester.

The first class, graduated in 1883, made the biggest impact on the stage, for little Jessie Bonesteele became a great name in the American theatre. Others in her class got jobs, but not the fame, met their mates and never moved back to Fishers. Those who did not move away were good public speakers, singers and added talent to the various organizations.

Jessie Bonesteele came from the town of Greece, where her parents owned a farm on what is now known as Bonesteele

Street; other streets were named for Jessie and her sister, Bernice. Jessie lived with her cousins next door to Valentown Hall in the Bonesteele cobblestone house.

Jessie organized a theatrical stock company and herself trained many hopeful young people. One was eight year old Mary Pickford who became America's first movie star. Some of her other students who gained stardom were Melvin Douglas, Ann Harding, Catherine Cornell, Minor Watson, Katherine Alexander, Gail Sandergaard and many more. Our Valentown register lists a number of Jessie's student associates who came here to see where Jessie got her training. Jessie had her own dramatic theatre in Detroit which is now owned by Wayne State University. Her company traveled far and was very popular during her time. One thing that she learned at Valentown and insisted upon was "at all times be yourself." When she was to see her brother for the first time in many years, she fussed as to how dramatic she should be. When they met, she just said, "Hello." Jessie kept in touch for many years with her Fishers friends. When I reopened Valentown Hall, several of Jessie's graduating class members repeated a dramatical scene which they gave in 1883.

C. W. Richardson's School of Acting created somewhat of a boom in plays and debates. The Valentown Grange presentd such plays as, *The Old Dairy Homestead, The Irish Washer Woman, The Octoroon, The Scarlet Letter, The Wife's Secret, The Babes in the Wood, East Lynne, A Modern Anaias,* and *Hans Von Smash.*

The Independent Order of Good Templars, a temperance group, also put on plays, which listed, *Ten Nights in a Barroom, Among the Breakers, The Muskeegan Nigger, A Little More Cider, We're All Teetotallers, Seeing the Elephant,* and *The Little Brown Jug.* The temperance people all wore a blue ribbon as abstainers from alcoholic beverages. Those who patronized the Fishers Hotel

Saloon wore red ribbons. Each group challenged the other to a weekly ball game, which kept a good community spirit.

The Benson School of Art

Abbie Benson of Benson Road rented a room on the second floor of Valentown Hall when it was built in 1879. She offered advanced classes in landscape and china painting taught by hired neighbors who lived on Main Street, members of the Parks family, as teachers. There were classes in making wax flowers and fruit, painting on velvet and drawings. Some of this work is still tucked away in local attics.

John Parks was a noted portrait artist who would stay at the home of a wealthy family until all of the members were painted. Alice Parks, a musician and artist, had studios in New York and Chicago. She was commissioned by the Vanderbilts and other wealthy New Yorkers to paint their table china. Sister Charlotte Parks, who married Reece Reed, did work in oil and also did china painting. Daughter Vera Reed did the same. Lucy Bushman Fisher did painting on velvet and flowers and fruit in wax.

Valentown School of Business

For several years Professor Julian Morris from Wayland conducted a school of business in Valentown Hall. The two-year course included all modern business methods, shorthand, banking, insurance, real estate, accounting and the social graces of society. The first graduating class numbered sixteen. Levi Valentine, who also was a student, was told that he should have taken the business course first and then he would have never built Valentown Hall.

In the cobblestone schoolhouse nearby was a teacher Levi was courting by the name of Hannah Payne. The schoolchildren wrote this poem:

> "Levi Valentine is a Granger. Building is his greatest danger. Hannah Payne can teach him better, if he's wise enough to get her."

He didn't get her.

Unfortunately, the surveyed railroad—the Pittsburgh Shawmut and Northern—ran out of money for construction when still 40 miles to the south. Valentown businesses withered, and Levi soon lost his property.

Levi's brother, Alanson, also had a financial interest in Valentown. The two brothers split up, when the property was lost, and the descendants never got back together. Alanson's side of the family called Valentown "Levi's Folly," the name was also used by others.

For 30 years the grocery stayed open and some functions were held in the ballroom, but the building was empty for the next 30 years. I had a special sentiment for the building because my mother and father met here in a play in 1905. Many others also met their mates at social events here. When demolition was planned in 1940, I purchased the property to create a museum, featuring an early shopping plaza, to be known as the "Ghost Town of Valentown."

Ichabod Town's, Samuel Valentine's and Levi Valentine's dreams of a shopping center adjacent to their farm were realized in 1970 when Eastview Mall, the largest enclosed shopping plaza between New York City and Cleveland at that time, was built across Route 96 and within sight of Valentown Hall.

Sarah and Margaret Murphy

The Night The Arsenal Was Raided

The Civil War had drained 5,000 men out of Ontario County leaving only young boys, older men and those rejected for military service. In Fishers this group was organized, for possible emergencies, into a home guard called the Goose Rangers.

The captain was Charles Murphy, who had served for six years as a British Army officer and was now a foreman on the New York Central Railroad. Captain Murphy's two sons were members of the Goose Rangers prior to joining active service in the Union Army. Sylvester became a troop train conductor for the north and participated in the southern campaigns. Sylvester survived but there was a loss of life when his troop train was wrecked on the curve just east of the Fishers station. The baggage car carried hundreds of dollars in silver for the soldier's pay, some of which has been found recently with metal detectors. His brother Thomas was a Union officer and his sword is in the Valentown Museum.

Captain Murphy also had two tomboy daughters—Sarah and Margaret, who was always known as "Maggie." They kept Fishers in an uproar with their youthful capers and in their later years they enjoyed telling me about some of them. Their most successful caper was when they played upon the hysteria generated by the rumored Confederate invasion through Canada.

The Northern states had been free from worry until Lee invaded Pennsylvania south of Gettysburg; then everyone became jittery. Using the disguise of tourists from Canada, a Confederate unit had captured a ship on Lake Erie. Again on October 19, 1864, another Rebel unit raided St. Albans, Vermont, robbed a bank and escaped back into Canada. After this, the army and all home guards were on full alert and the forts along Lake Erie, Lake Ontario and the St. Lawrence River were all reinforced. Locally the people felt vulnerable for trouble because Fishers' Wilder Wagon Company was making cannon carriages and caissons for the Union army.

The big scare came a week after the St. Albans raid. One midnight Sarah and Maggie and their farm girl friends, using

Arthur "General" C. C. Hamlitz
Courted Sarah Murphy but she did not
"see eye to eye with him."

horses, hauled the local arsenal's four cannons up on the hills overlooking Fishers. For awhile they set cannon fire—minus the cannonballs. The Goose Rangers assembled at Captain Murphy's house next to the railroad station. They were very reluctant to make a charge on any of the batteries for the lack of knowledge of the force opposing them. Telegraph messages for help were sent to Rochester, Canandaigua and Camp Swift in Geneva saying that the Rebels from Canada were attacking.

Never before nor since has such panic struck the community. It seemed that there was no escape; the people seemed surrounded. Those who were fortunate enough to have outside underground root or potato cellars gave refuge to as many neighbors as they could hold, while others hid out in their house cellars.

During the early morning hours, military units from other towns began organizing and moved towards the supposed point of attack in Fishers. At daybreak the counterattackers found no Rebel-Confederates, only unmanned cannons owned by Fishers' own Goose Rangers.

Sarah Murphy's granddaughter, "Diff" Snyder, often told me that Sarah told her that she had also fired off several rounds in the yard of Charles "Squire" Fisher because he did not like loud noises.

The Indomitable Welch Family

When the Auburn and Rochester Railroad was constructed through Fishers in 1838, two gravel roads were in use on each side of the tracks between the railroad station and Phillips Road. On the east side of the tracks it was Tipperary Road and on the west it was Shamrock Lane.

Among the families who lived on the east side were Tim Daley, John Regan, Morris Leahy and Thomas Donahue. Those living on the west side numbered about 25 families, including John McCarthy, Widow Welch and Thomas Burns, whose house foundations are still visible.

Widow Welch made history when the trains began running in 1840. The top speed of the trains was ten miles an hour, and wood was the fuel used for the engines. One train going east on the upgrade past her house ran out of wood by her woodpile. The fireman took enough wood to get to the next railroad woodpile. The next day she met the train at the station and demanded pay for the stolen wood, but she was refused. To compound the widow's problems, the train killed her pig. Again she demanded payment, and again they refused her.

A new industry like the railroad, should be given a lesson in public relations, the widow Welch felt. On its next trip east as the passenger train came along blowing its shrill whistle, the high locomotive drive wheels began to spin with no forward traction. The widow Welch had greased the tracks and the conductor had to borrow money from the passengers to pay widow Welch for the pig and the wood. Widow Welch had made her point and the section crew under Charles "Boss" Murphy, who lived next to the station, was called to clean and sand the tracks in order to get the train underway again.

Timothy Welch lived on the northeast corner of Log Cabin Road and Main Street, Fishers. He considered himself a very practical man who, if anything went wrong, would thereafter do the opposite so that the same thing would not happen again. However, his family and friends felt that sometimes doing the opposite was carrying his theory too far.

One situation which happened to him shouldn't happen to anybody. While hurrying through the barn in the dark, he turned left and slipped and fell flat into a pool of semi-liquid manure. He vowed to never turn left again. For the rest of his life he maintained that obsession. He solved the problem of turning left by turning right, thus making a complete right turnabout.

Wherever Timothy went, he attracted much attention. In church he caused confusion. A sudden right turnabout for getting to the equivalent of a left turn into a pew often would catch a stranger off guard and trip him. Eventually, a right side pew in the back row was assigned to him.

One time while shopping in Rochester he was doing his right turnabouts before entering each store so much so that he attracted the attention of the police. He was held at the police station long enough for a check to be made at the State Hospital to see if a patient had escaped. He explained the reasons for his actions to the satisfaction of the police and was let go.

A passenger train brakeman once noticed his gyrations at the Rochester station and barred him from boarding the train home but the conductor knew him and allowed him to board. He has gone down in local history as a colorful figure known as "Right-

Turn-Welch."

"Yankee" Welch was another colorful figure who worked on the railroad as a crossing flagman.

The 1845 Cobblestone Pump House at Fishers.
Edward Hungerford, Vice-president of the New York Central Railroad and noted railroad historian, who helped save the building in 1937, and J. Sheldon Fisher, Victor Historian.

The Ice-Climbing Locomotive

One would think that a huge freight locomotive could crush its way through a patch of ice on the tracks. No so, for I saw an engine try to do it unsuccessfully.

The setting for this event was at the Fishers railroad station. There were three tracks between the station and the cobblestone pumphouse. A freight train had taken the long siding next to the pumphouse but had stopped a short distance on its way west. An eastbound passenger train was due any minute. The section boss and his workers had declared an emergency because chunks of ice had plugged the raceway going under the pumphouse to the millpond beyond.

Water, overflowing the raceway onto the tracks and Main Street, was freezing in the sub-zero weather. The section gang could not cope with so much ice and pressed into service several able-bodied youths to chop the ice away as they cleared the ice from the pumphouse intake. We chopped the ice from the main tracks sufficiently to get the passenger train through.

Now that the mainline was clear to Pittsford, the freight train got overly anxious to leave. We chopped as hard as we could, but the ice was too thick. The engineer told us to get off the track, for he was going through. Several of us stood on the main track to see what would happen. The four-wheel pony truck next to the cow-catcher started to climb up the ice, which raised the front drive wheels off the track.

What amazed me was that the engineer didn't seem to know that the ice was not being crushed under the wheels. The engine started to tip towards us! Someone tripped me trying to get out of the way. It didn't matter—as the freight train moved ahead, it tipped the other way against the pumphouse. We heard a scream from a section man, who seemed to be pinned between the engine and the pumphouse. By that time the engineer had shut off the steam, because he was off the track, and he stayed off for four or five hours. Fortunately, the man was not injured and was more scared than hurt. A wrecking train came from the Rochester yard with a powerful hoist and eventually moved the locomotive backwards onto the track again while another crew of men were brought in to chop the ice from the tracks and the hand operated switches.

It was a sight that I had never expected to see and one that I could never forget. Ever after I have had a soft spot in my heart for the 1845 pumphouse for having the locomotive fall on it instead of me. In 1937, the New York Central Railroad issued an order to demolish the cobblestone building. I fought hard to save it and even got the vice-president of the railroad to come from New York City to investigate. He went to the chairman of the board, who then issued an order to save it as an historic landmark.

It stands today a symbol of the bygone era of the steam locomotive.

The Schoolhouse
That Wouldn't Stay Put

So often school boards, teachers, budgets and schoolhouses are the center of a community uproar. Usually the problems are solved within a school year and everything goes along peacefully. Not so with the Fishers School District. Their controversy lasted over 80 years, with bitter disputes all at the expense of the children, although they never took sides. Fortunately, there never was any bloodshed. It all came down to the simple fact that two families a mile apart wanted the schoolhouse nearest their farms so that their children didn't have to walk so far.

The first Fishers schoolhouse was an abandoned log blockhouse fort, which had been originally built in 1792 as one of a series of forts built in anticipation of Indian trouble. According to the record, it was located in the southeast corner of lot number 40 of the 11th township of the 4th range of the Phelps and Gorham Purchase of Western New York. Today it is better known as the site of the processing building for Sharp's Honey Farm on Fisher Road. The location was selected because it was a strategic spot overlooking a sweeping view of the once navigable Irondequoit Creek.

After the signing of the Pickering Treaty between the United States Government and the Iroquois Indians at Canandaigua in 1794, peace was declared and all danger ended.

The fort was then used as a public meeting place, a school on weekdays, and a church on Sunday.

The very location of the structure being on the north side of the school district brought objections from some of the parents on the southside of the district. By 1826 the antagonism of the southsiders had heated up so much that the building burned under mysterious circumstances.

From the minutes, six special school meetings were held before a new log blockhouse was again built. The general opinion was to rebuild on district land and not on the southside. Asa Gaskill offered a new building site for $25.00, but it was rejected. At the meeting on May 19, 1827, it was resolved to build on the same site, the same as the previous structure, 20 feet square, with a brick chimney and a board roof. A later meeting called for a shingled roof. The meetings stood with the October 6, 1824 resolution, which called for each inhabitant to furnish one half cord of wood for the fire for each scholar sent to school. If anyone failed to furnish wood, they had to pay eighty-seven and a half cents per cord. For the winter of 1829–30, William Woolston was paid $50 for teaching in the blockhouse school.

Because of the increasing population, a compromise was made to reduce the size of the school district and build a structure in the center area. It was to be known as Wanghum Seminary. The northern section had included Slab Hollow, later called Railroad Mills. This area was transferred into Monroe County to form a new district #15 to include parts of the Towns of Mendon and Pittsford. This reduction was made to stop the schoolhouse burnings.

The seminary building was declared hastily built and not suitable for use. On January 26, 1838, it was ordered to be nearly all rebuilt. The outside was to be painted "Venetian Read" (sic) with white trim.

The school building had no space for a library. It was agreed that Erastus Ford continue to be the librarian, although he lived a mile from the school. On October 7, 1834, he acknowledged receipt of 37 new books, including *Life of Washington, Life of Cromwell, Manual of Politeness, Beecher on Temperance* and *Indian Wars.*

In 1838 the school received from the state books and a wooden box, complete with shelves and a hinged door. These books were of standard size, four inches by six inches, marked on the binding "School District Library." In order to get the books the district had to match $10 towards the $20 cost of the fifty titles selected for common school districts. The New York State Legislature appropriated $40,000 for the state-wide program.

The change in the location of the schoolhouse still did not satisfy those residents further south. That faction, headed by Lysander and Jerome Hill, called school meetings without notifying the taxpayers in the northern section. Their purpose was to raise money to build another schoolhouse nearer the southern border of the district, supported by the Hill party. First they set up a private school which met in private homes. This was opposed by the Collins party headed by George S. Collins on Phillips Road over on the east side of the district.

Tension increased. A tug of war—or rather a "tug of the schoolhouse"—took place every so often during the 1850s and 1860s. Teams of mules moved the schoolhouse north down the hill during the night from the present site of Rochester Block Company to the site of Larry Fisher's house. When the Collins party was off guard, back the building would go up the hill on another dark night. This happened frequently.

"Uncle" Johnny Hailey and other residents used to tell me about the fun they had when they were students with their midnight rides in the old schoolhouse up and down the hill.

On the night of May 15, 1864, several days after the building was moved back up the hill, somebody burned down the schoolhouse. The Fishers community was shocked and angered. Charles Fisher, Asa Wiley, John McCarthy, Herman and Henry Van Voorhis headed a subscription list to raise money for a temporary school building. The building was to be placed near the railroad station for protection. The building has gone down in history as the "Shanty Schoolhouse." Charles Fisher's sister-in-law, Alice D. Pardee, was paid $60 a year for two years to teach here.

For several years both sides had been pleading with the New York State Superintendent of Schools for mediation, but nothing ever came of it. The Hill Party petitioned the state to declare their new schoolhouse next to Jerome's house the official building instead of the Shanty Schoolhouse. On March 6, 1867, it was voted to buy the building and move it to the old site, down the hill. A great amount of haggling continued until it was agreed to move the building back up the hill. By 1912 an enlarged population called for more classroom space. A concrete block building was constructed down the hill, one that could not be moved, which was used until the district was centralized in 1940. The old schoolhouse ended its days as a storage building for hay. Vandals set it afire at three o'clock in the afternoon on April 22, 1923.

I saved the old room-wide recitation bench carved with initials, on which my grandfather, my father, myself and all of my brothers and sisters and relatives sat. I also have the old hand bell saved by the teacher, Frances Pardee Blackman, when the first schoolhouse burned in 1864.

Young men who worked on farms went to school during the cold winter months and often created serious problems for the women teachers. Fathers with immigrant children would also attend school at that time. It was common for the teachers to be thrown out in the snow by the husky boys. One problem was solved by hiring an expert fighter as the teacher. I remember hearing how the boys grabbed the new male teacher, only to find themselves well battered in a pile of snow themselves.

The village prankster was Charles H. Fisher and he was one all of his life. He told how he drilled a hole in the floor at his desk and under the floor ran a cord to the front door and attached it to a hinged door knocker. At an opportune time he would pull the cord and make a knocking sound. When the teacher got there, no one could be found. Long before the building burned I crawled through the broken foundation and found the ingenious device.

After telling about all of these old-time school capers, I will admit that, in a low-key manner, I did my share such as filling the teacher's desk drawers with mice. I liked to see her climb up on the desk and call for help.

The Lightning Calculator

In the 1870s, Jonathan W. Phillips' grocery store was the place to congregate for those men who did not partronize the Fishers Hotel saloon. It was the place to exchange the latest news and gossip.

Fortunately, the store was big enough to accomodate the buyers and non-buyers. Benches and heavy wooden chairs were arranged around the big old stove. Often someone would bring a mouth organ and play a few tunes. Some who could sing would even harmonize. Of course there were also those Civil War veterans who liked to recount how they had won the war.

One bit of entertainment was reserved to impress the out-of-town visitors. That was the mental exploits of Michael Connelly, known as the "Lightning Calculator." Mike, as he was normally called, could listen to any number of figures and immediately give the total of the numbers presented. This was also true of subtraction, multiplication, and division. Many hours were spent in the store trying to trip up Mike on his calculations, but to no avail.

Many people quizzed Mike on how he became so good in mathematics since he had only an elementary school education, and not much of that, in County Cork, Ireland. He came here with his wife during the potato famine. He would always pass it off by saying that it was only a gift.

The Irish came here because they could get jobs on the

railroad. While others took manual labor, Mike got an office job in the station. As his fame spread, he took on all kinds of mathematical work, including balancing business books here and in nearby towns. He would take the train daily to audit the books of Rochester banks. He was pressed into being a showman to put on demonstrations at county fairs, clubs, church socials and other public gatherings. He helped his son, John Connelly, to establish himself in Fishers as a produce commission merchant.

The foundations of the Michael Connelly house have just about vanished on Log Cabin Road. Years ago I gave in to my curiosity, and I dug around the spot and found the usual objects, such as broken dishes, metal items, and two perfect Irish smoking pipes. While I was digging I wondered how a person could acquire such a mental gift.

The 1790 Log Cabin

Unusual Animals and Birds

The Postal Raccoon

James R. Weichbrodt was born more than 80 years ago. He was brought up in the 1790 log cabin at the end of Log Cabin Road and he roamed the fields and woods as a young lad. The wild animals became his playmates. He befriended woodchucks, skunks, raccoons and foxes. When the animals learned that he meant them no harm, they would go to him for food and to be scratched. They would even follow him home and romp with his cats and dog. As he got older he would go to Rochester and walk in public places with a raccoon on his shoulders and a fox on a leash. All of his life he was known as "Jimmy Woodchuck."

One day when he was in the Fishers post office the raccoon jumped through the mail wicket and landed on a black-inked stamp pad. It then walked over mail and post office reports leaving footprints all over everything. The head office wrote back to find out if they were short of cancelling devices and what the postmaster was now using. The postmaster, W. A. Lewis, replied that he now had a raccoon to speed up stamp cancelling for faster mail service!

Square Dancing Pigs

Jim Sullivan on Fisher Road had his own private circus to

show his friends. Three young pigs were trained to dance to phonograph music. They would do rolls, jump over each other and do square dance figures.

Two Local Beggers

Joe Barnes and his wife lived on Wangum Road before World War I. They had a horse which was fond of candy and chewing tobacco. They also had a talking crow. Both horse and crow were fast friends. The crow liked meat scraps and oysters. The two would go on a begging trip together to Fowler's store and then to Jones' store with the crow riding on the horse.

The crow would beat its wings on the store door and call to attract attention. The crow's words were somewhat understandable, and besides, everyone knew what they wanted. The store customers would pay for the goodies just to watch the two enjoy the handouts. When the five o'clock whistle blew at the tile factory, the crow would fly over there and say to Mr. Barnes, "Joe, get the cows." The crow would be rewarded with a dish of fresh milk at chore time.

The Opera Singing Chicken

At the Fisher homestead we had a very unusual Blue Leghorn chicken with songs like no visitor had ever heard. It was nothing like any ordinary happy chicken singing in a well-fed flock.

We named the friendly chicken after the famous Swedish singer, Jenny Lind, who toured the United States in the 1850s. Before our Jenny burst into one of her songs, she would do a little vocalizing like they do in opera practice; then would come a long flow of beautiful musical notes. At daybreak Jenny would wake us up with her happy songs, which continued all day.

Professional showmen and singers actually beat a path to our door to hear Jenny sing. They all tried to buy her with tempting sums of money. My parents said no because Jenny was a member of our family and no member of our family was for sale. Jenny's songs were recorded on a phonograph cylinder, but we were never able to get a copy. However, we still had Jenny.

One night our chicken house was raided, and most of our chickens were stolen, but not Jenny, for she had a favorite roost high in the Maiden Blush apple tree at the end of our house. Other attempts were made to steal Jenny, but she lived a good, long happy chicken life, and when she died, we buried her at the base of her favorite apple tree. With all of the musicians and chicken experts who came to hear our Jenny, not one could explain how an ordinary chicken could have such a musical voice.

Pete The Tom Cat

Another Fisher homestead character was Pete, a big tiger tom cat, who seemed to live just to kill snakes. He was very proud of this accomplishment and made it a point to draw praise by dragging the dead snakes to our back steps and wait for acknowledgment and a food reward before leaving on another hunt. We named him "Pete" after Rochester's famed "Rattlesnake Pete" Gruber who had a saloon and adjoining museum of curiosities with cages of snakes.

When my sister Ella was a baby, she played in the back yard. Suddenly, one day, a great commotion arose with the robins, bluebirds, and chickens raising a great fuss. A big snake was crawling towards the baby. Pete appeared just as my distraught mother did. Pete, with one bound, clamped his teeth into the neck of the snake and killed it. Pete lived as a hero at our house for many years.

Milk Thieves

The Gutberlet dairy farm bordering our farm on the west was in a beautiful shade area along Irondequoit Creek. It was a favorite resting place for the cows during the heat of the day. There had been losses of cattle in the area and cattle rustlers were suspect for anything that was mislaid or missing around the farm.

A problem arose when it was discovered the cow's milk was short on some days and not on others. Farm help was hidden in the bushes nearby to watch the cows to see if anyone was milking the cows and taking it away. Even though no person was seen near the cows the milkings were unduly short. One day one of the men walked among the cows while they were lying down and found a mess of snakes sucking milk from the cows. It has long been known that cows allow snakes to milk them when their udder is under pressure; this may be how the variety of Milk Snake got its name.

The cows were removed to another pasture and pigs were fenced in at the spot to kill off the snakes.

Railroad Highlights

The halfway post of the Auburn and Rochester Railroad, between Fishers and Pittsford, was located at the point where Park Road intersects East Street. When the trains began running in the 1840s, there were no communications between stations on a one-track road. As it was done on all rail lines, trains headed towards each other, the one reaching the post first had the right-of-way. The loser had to back up to the station it had just left. The halfway post was the cause of many head-on collisions.

* * *

The Liberty Bell was on the Fishers siding on November 24, 1915. Since I always looked at every train that went by our house, I was surprised to see this special train with a flat car with our Liberty Bell mounted in the center. Our whole family hurried up the street, along with many others, to get a closer look at the bell. We learned that it had been on display at the San Francisco World's Fair and was now on its way back to Philadelphia.

* * *

The great trolley and train race made world history when the new electric trolley was pitted against a steam train to see which was the fastest. It was a four-mile race on parallel tracks from Maple Avenue in Victor to Main Street in Fishers after the

trolley tracks were completed between Geneva and Rochester in 1904.

Engineer Ford, better known as "Fordy," was an Auburn Road engineer with as much daring as the legendary Casey Jones. He was considered by his associates as a speed demon and one who belonged on the straight tracks of the Main Line, and certainly not on the winding tracks of the Auburn Road. The distances between stations were short, and this fact probably kept

Fordy's engines from jumping the tracks more often.

Fordy had a good head of steam when the flagman let the two-car train and the trolley leave the Victor station at the same time. Photographers were waiting at the Swamp Road crossing, and at that point the trolley was taking the lead. The fireman was shoveling the coal as fast as he could, and Fordy had the throttle wide open. The whistle was not even blown at the crossing in order to conserve steam; guards kept vehicles at a safe distance.

The trolley car had a disadvantage in that it had to climb the steep grade over the Lehigh Valley Railroad tracks, while the steam train had a straight and level stretch to Fishers. At the Lehigh tracks the racers' course veered apart. Signal cannon were placed at each Main Street station. Halfway between the stations men were located with stop watches waiting for the signals. The exact time has been forgotten, but the trolley did win.

It was Eddy Dwyer as motorman, of the Rochester and Eastern Rapid Railway, pitted against Engineer Ford that day and for years after they would race when they found themselves going in the same direction. Eddy Dwyer gave me the official photo of that famous race, along with his hat and badge when he retired.

On another occasion, Fordy overstepped the train rules one day when he came roaring from the east ahead of schedule. He did not allow a freight train going east enough time to clear the main track to a siding at Fishers. Two freight cars still on the main track were knocked into the lumber mill yard. Fordy got a light reprimand.

* * *

A coal train derailed across Main Street in Fishers in 1905 spreading coal over a good stretch of the tracks. Many coal bins had not yet been filled for the winter. Word of the wreck spread rapidly over the countryside, and a parade of wagons converged on the station. People came with pails, wheelbarrows and pushcarts, and they took what they could back home.

The seven o'clock passenger train arrived and was shunted around the wreck by way of the team track. The train was delayed at the station for about 15 minutes, which gave Charlie Fisher time enough to pull off another one of his famous pranks.

Putting on a good disguise, he got on the end of the train and walked through the cars and got off with the passengers. With a pad and pencil, he began asking the names of those taking coal. This little act panicked those gathering coal and many left in a hurry with nothing. Charlie scored again.

* * *

An unauthorized flying switch came close to being a catastrophe in the summer of 1916 at Fishers. Concerned in this episode were two freight trains. An eastbound local train, with orders to keep off the main track, was on the long siding placing various cars at different industries. A fast freight train was due from Canandaigua to Rochester with perishable southern fruits and watermelons. Nothing was to interfere with this special express.

While the engineer had gone to the privy behind the station, the fireman, who wanted to be an engineer, took it upon himself to place a few cars on the sidings for those who wanted them. The cars designated for these spots had to be cut out of the train. A brakeman was at the switch. Another brakeman rode the car to be switched. The locomotive towing that car would travel at a moderate speed. Just before reaching the siding the brakeman would cut the car loose and the locomotive would speed up past the switch, so that it could be opened and the riding brakeman would lock the brakes by turning the control wheel on the top end of the car thus bringing it to a stop on the siding and keeping it from rolling back to the main track. This maneuver was called making a "flying switch" and this tactic was almost always perfectly safe when the brakemen did their job by securing the brakes.

The fireman, having a happy time being an engineer after

placing the car, blissfully headed his locomotive up the main track towards the express special, which was blasting away on its whistle. The errant fireman suddenly saw with horror that he was due for a head on collision. He threw the engine into reverse, opened the throttle to full speed, and jumped. They hit, but with no greater impact than to damage the protruding cow catchers, those grill-like plows made to throw off animals and vehicles from derailing trains.

As I have heard it told, a great hubbub arose around the station, dominated by the yelling, cursing engineer, whose locomotive was being used. The engine had became a runaway, going at top speed, headed for Pittsford. Everyone was terribly worried that the engine would jump the tracks at Baldwin's curve on the other side of Railroad Mills.

The fruit train, with the local engineer now on board,

The run-a-way locomotive brought back to Fishers.
Fishers station agent, William Stanley, is 4th from left.

tagged the runaway almost to Pittsford, where it ran out of steam; he returned it to Fishers. The fireman's railroad career ended the moment he jumped and left town.

One day I was standing by the lumber mill watching this same kind of operation when the switched car didn't stay put. It rolled back, out of control, towards the closed main track switch. A car being pushed ahead of the locomotive and the rolling car met end to end and both went up into the air deadlocked. I yelled to the engineer before it happened, but he didn't hear or just ignored me. Heavy sawed timbers from the mill were used to pry the cars free of each other.

New York Central Freight House at Fishers, NY
Charles W. Ford & Co. warehouse in background

A jinxed barrel of molasses, weighing over 500 pounds, should have never been taken lightly. Charles Riley was a brakeman on the local freight trains. He was one of those muscular exhibits weighing around 300 pounds. When the trains were headed home, the men always wanted to hasten their work so that they could get home early. Instead of cutting out the LCLs (Less Car Lots) box cars from the train to unload at the freight house, often they preferred to carry the goods across the siding to do so. They would load the heaviest things on Riley's back.

One afternoon he started across the tracks with a barrel of molasses on his back when his heel caught in the rail and he fell. The weight of the barrel crushed his chest, and he died.

The barrel of molasses was later rolled over to Fowler's Store. While George Proseus and Fred Fowler were slowly rolling the barrel down the steps into the cellar, it broke away and crashed into the cellar wall, emptying its contents all over the floor. Thus ended a jinxed barrel of molasses.

* * *

A southern watermelon train took the long siding at Fishers late one afternoon headed for Rochester. A few of us young folks were canoeing in the raceway along the tracks. One of the brakemen began tossing watermelons into the water for us before they moved on. There was hardly a youth for miles around who didn't get sick of watermelons because they had consumed so much. It was not only the taste for melons that was lost that year but also for bananas. A truck of bananas lost half of its load going up the Main Street hill and never came back.

Hobos

Every non-winter day for years, many hobos riding the freight trains would get off at the west yard switch and go to one of the Fishers stores for food and then to the grove near the tracks, not far from our house, to cook. At times some would come over to our back door for a bite to eat and a glass of buttermilk. Nearby we had a woodpile. My mother would hand an ax to the men to split wood to pay for the meal; she was never turned down. I enjoyed talking to the hobos; they loved to tell of their escapades and adventures in many places. I concluded that it was much too tough a life for me to ever try it.

One man claimed that he was the king of the hobos and that once a year it was his job to hold a convention in some convenient city. The king showed me the strange symbols cut into the supports of the water tower at the Fishers station and found at every other railroad station. These gave the transients information as to what to expect from the people of that town, and whether or not they were friendly. I copied them. Some resemble the well-known Pennsylvania hex marks.

Around the year 1900, Town Justice Robert Fisher was tired of burglaries and attempted train robberies by suspects brought before his court. He ordered the local constable to arrest on sight any hobo on a vagrancy charge. Gregory Hill said that the constable would give him a dime, when he was a boy, to warn the hobos down at the cooking grove of their impending arrest. Then by the time the constable arrived, the hobos were gone.

Mail Time

The ideal hub of a rural community once was composed of the railroad station, the post office, the grocery store, and the hotel. These were the places to feel the pulse of the outside world when trains arrived. It was this way for many years here as long as the trains ran.

Before the turn of the century, twenty-four passenger trains a day and eight freight trains stopped at Fishers. For the next twenty years there were only fourteen passenger and mail trains. The arrivals were so accurate that clocks were set by them. On looking back now, the scenes were like movie sets. Many horses were pulling wagons, buckboard and democrat wagons, surreys, and buggies with movable tops.

I always anticipated the reaction of the horses when the locomotives came-up hissing steam and belching black smoke. I could relate to the horses, because in my very early youth I was always terribly panicked when boarding a train and for years it gave me nightmares.

Many horses bolted wagons with and ran away. A husky woman from near Deadman's Curve had her horse race in circles out of control, and she was thrown out when the buggy overturned. Another woman weighing about three hundred and fifty pounds had come to the mill for ground feed. Her horse was frightened by a hissing locomotive. The horse reared up and jumped forward, throwing the woman backwards upside down

Mrs. Bessie C. Fisher, Postmaster, carrying the mail to Post Office from the Fishers railroad station. Extreme right is a freight car cutting out view of freight house. Foregound is the potato scales. Sattel's store at left. A short time later lightning shattered the flag pole and threw splinters all around her.

over the seat, landing with her feet up in the air. I helped catch the horse, but it took several men to return her to the buggy seat.

About fifteen of us young fellows had farm horses which we also used in stunt riding. Our audiences were often the passengers on the trains when they stopped near by. Some of us could hang over the horses' sides and pick up handkerchiefs from the ground and most could jump from one trotting horse to another.

At mail time the post office was overcrowded, and the customers had to be wary of the tobacco chewers who had to have good clearance when aiming at the open stove door. Very few missed their spitting aim from their seats around the stove. If one wanted sound knowledge of the real state of the nation, the post office was the place to hear it debated. In July, 1881, when President Garfield was shot by Charles Guiteau, it was one man's opinion that Guiteau deserved a good kick in the rear.

110

I could never figure out why the brakemen on the freight trains could never seem to remember that the heavy iron water spout was close to the tracks and a real danger. It was on the opposite side of the tracks from the water tower, which provided water for the steam locomotives. Over the years about nine men were killed here when they hung out at arm's length while shifting the freight cars.

Brakeman Tom O'Brien ran down the hill from his home when late for work and tried to catch on a slow moving freight train. He missed his grasp, fell between the cars, and one of his legs was cut off. "Uncle" Johnny Hailey, the crossing flagman, pulled Tom free. Tom continued to work for the railroad with his wooden leg. He lived out his life in Fishers with his brothers, Mike and Bill, who for years was the station agent.

Fowlers Store in Fishers.
Fred G. Fowler, left, Mrs. Addie Fowler, his mother, Betty Fowler, Bud Fowler and Bessie C. Fisher, Postmaster. Fishers Post Office is at left; railroad water tank shows at right.

The Auburn Road of the New York Central was like a good neighbor. The conductors and brakemen performed many little courtesies for Fishers residents. Grocery stores and meat markets in Rochester with specials would take our orders, deliver them to the Rochester Station to be picked up at the Fishers station. Coffee and a full cooky jar was always available at the nearby homes for the railroad men when they made deliveries directly to the house as happened often in the 1920s.

The passenger trains, which all stopped here, were our window to the outside world. All of the telegraph operators from Rochester to Syracuse knew when there were celebrities on the trains, including the one at Fishers, giving us a chance to see them. Jess Willard, Jack Johnson, Ty Cobb, Walter Johnson, William Jennings Bryan, and Charles Evans Hughes came through Fishers. The last notable was President Harry Truman, who in his whistlestop election campaign, came in the sleekest, streamlined train ever to ride the local rails.

Conover and Conover

The rugged hills in the southern part of the Town of Perinton in 1840 seemed to be the most unlikely place to start any kind of business. They rise to about 1,000 feet above sea level and plunge to valleys and ragged cliffs. This terrible but beautiful glaciated terrain was actually a part of a thriving business centered here and which stretched west to the Mississippi River.

Two locally-born brothers, William J. and Van Rensselaer Conover, started a livestock business and bought several hundred acres and leased several hundred more of this difficult-to-farm hill country for pasture. The area became known as Conover Hills. Today it is known as Turk Hill and Baker Hill.

This became the headquarters for a wide-reaching project to support the flow of livestock from the west to the New York City market. New towns were built in different states, settled by local New York State people, and run by the Conover brothers and their cousins. Near these new towns, gathering centers were located from which sheep and cattle were driven to the Fishers area and Conover Hills for fattening before taking them on to the New York City market. The several hundred men who were employed to handle the stock were called drovers, the forerunners of cowboys. The drovers had a more difficult job weaving their herds around towns than did the plains cowboys. Upon purchase, the Conover "C" brand was put on the animals with red paint. The branding irons and other accessories are in

Samuel Conover

the collection at the Valentown Museum.

The business operation became so big and extended that the work had to be divided up. William took over the department on sheep and was called "Mutton" Conover. Van Rensselaer handled the cattle and was called "Beef" Conover. Much of the financing was done by Van Rensselaer's father-in-law, Gershom Dunham of Fairport, who with his wife, Cynthia, furnished the first mail service between Rochester and Canandaigua on horseback, and by a third wealthy brother, Samuel S. Conover, who was developing Milwaukee, Wisconsin.

Samuel took time to scout the neighboring states to find out where it would be feasible to establish animal collecting centers.

Van Rensselaer Conover

Because test runs by drovers with sheep and cattle from Minnesota and Wisconsin to the Conover Hills proved to be too difficult, no centers were established there.

William J. Conover wanted to establish a collecting center in Virginia and found a suitable tract of land near Petersburg. Samuel visited the farm on January 24, 1853, and found that it was an ideal piece of property. However, it had many liens and a faulty title and he refused to buy it. Twelve years later, in 1865, it was the scene of one of the bloodiest battles of the Civil War. It was here that the Union soldiers dug a long tunnel under the Confederate camp and filled it with explosives. If the Conovers had bought that farm, they would have been left with a huge

William J. Conover

crater in the middle of their farm. In 1926 it became a National Military Park.

Temporary farm lands were rented in parts of Ohio and Indiana for holding animal purchases. Some additional land was rented in Pennsylvania which was suitable only for grazing by sheep as a result of Lyman Wilmarth's lumbering project which had left the area full of stumps. This served very well as one of William Conover's collecting centers.

Earlier James Ridgway, a Philadelphia financier, who owned a large tract of land in Elk County, Pennsylvania, had hired James Gillis of Victor to develop Ridgway, Pennsylvania. James married Ridgway's attractive daughter, Mary, and settled a new village

Sylvester Millard

with Victor people, thus making it a sister village of Victor, New York. George Dickinson went there and built a mansion, which is still standing at 106 West Main Street in Ridgway. His brother-in-law, Lyman Wilmarth, also from Boughton Hill, Victor, settled there, too, buying land west of Ridgway and establishing the post office village of Wilmarth, Pennsylvania, which was the center of his lumbering business. As his lumbering project was being completed, the area was left with stumps, making the land suitable only for sheep grazing. It was then used as another collecting center for William Conover.

James Gillis moved back to Victor with his wife, who soon died and was buried in the Victor Methodist Cemetery. James

Isaac Snedeker

took his secrecy vows in the Masonic order very seriously. When William Morgan published the secrets of Masonry in 1826, James Gillis was one of the men who abducted Morgan out of the Canandaigua jail and Morgan was never seen again. He was indicted for murder but nothing was ever proven. It created such a scandal that the Anti-Masonic Party was formed, with William Wirt as the United States Presidential candidate.

A Conover cousin, Isaac Snedeker, was sent to populate Jerseyville, Illinois, across the Mississippi River from St. Louis, Missouri. This was to be a cattle collecting center from the western cattle ranches. There was a strong family bond in Jerseyville because the Conover, Snedeker and Stout families were all descended from the prominent Stout family of New

Jersey. Later, James Gillis and other Perinton and Town of Victor people went to Jerseyville, where Gillis was to help buy cattle. He then went to Iowa to scout out the cattle buying possibilities and the feasibility of driving them back east, but it was decided to just stay with the Jerseyville operation. James died in Iowa.

Samuel S. Conover moved his business headquarters across Lake Michigan to Manistee, Michigan, where he arranged to acquire a large tract of land in Clinton County, north of Lansing, for a sheep collecting center. Settlers from Perinton, Victor, Fishers, Mendon, and East Bloomfield moved to the new tract. Cousin John Van Vechten was to buy sheep and arrange for the sheep facilities. To name the new Clinton County tract, hometown names were tossed around. The most vocal came from the Town of Victor people, so it became Victor, Michigan.

On July 1, 1847, a post office was established in Victor, Michigan, with Hugh Haggerty as postmaster. The next postmaster was Henry Buell from East Bloomfield, New York. A Victor, New York, Methodist, Daniel Blood, used his cabin to start a church of that denomination. The Brunsons, who were Congregationalists from East Bloomfield, started that church. The Reeds used the schoolhouse for the United Brethren Church. Samuel Treat from Mendon became the Town Supervisor. William A. Upton and his family were influential citizens as they had been in Victor, New York. After buying sheep for awhile, William Upton went to the State of Washington, where he became a Supreme Court Judge. Later he became Comptroller for the United States Treasury under President Lincoln.

The Conover brothers' stepfather, Samuel F. Millard, moved from Victor, New York to Victor, Michigan, to manage the business there. During college vacations his son, Sylvester, drove sheep to the Conover Hills. After college he became a

Chicago merchant and was one who was not wiped out by the great Chicago fire of 1871. He prospered well and became a collector of rare American art. Sylvester's grandson, Everett Millard, was my guest in Fishers in 1938, when he was taking a number of life and death masks of famous Americans to sell in New York City. They were purchased by the Clark family and given to the Farmers Museum in Cooperstown, where they can be seen today.

The Civil War provided a new opportunity for the Conover business. The Union Army of the west was capturing hundreds of mules from the Confederate Army and from farmers. Cousin Isaac Snedeker paid $50 a head, and the drovers flooded the pasture land around Fishers with mules. They were delivered back to the Union Army of the east as fast as broker E. B. Bishop in Jersey City could arrange their sale for $200 to $600 each, depending on their size and quality. This shows the lack of communications and organization in the Union Army. Many of the mules were also sold to western New York farmers. Letters show that at the same time Cousin Isaac was also buying hundreds of captured horses at $5 to $20 each and selling them to farmers and the Union Cavalry in the east.

Everything looked great for the future of Victor, Michigan, when the Grand Trunk Railroad surveyed a route through the village. But seven miles to the north the towns of St. Johns and Ovid together brought pressure on the railroad to change the route to go through their towns, which was done and so growth of Victor stopped. Samuel S. Conover had claimed he would not give a loan to anybody for less than $25,000. He wrote a letter back home saying he did not think that his brother, William J., "would ever be able to build Victor into a CITY in the west."

Old age and the strain of long distance business prompted

the sale of Victor, Michigan in 1883. Victor's identity is now gone and it does not show on present day maps. In 1880 Samuel F. Millard had moved back to the home of his stepson, Van Rensselaer Conover, on the Mason Road farm in Egypt, which joined the land of the Conover Hills. Van Rensselaer died in 1882. William J. died in 1892 and was buried in the cemetery behind the South Perinton Methodist Church near the Snedekers and many of his relatives. This is less than a mile from the site in the Town of Victor of the log cabin in which he was born and where his mother, Diadama Frederick Conover, killed a rattlesnake coiled around him in his crib in 1825.

In 1907 my mother, Bessie Conover Fisher, inherited a share of these hills from her father, Leander A. Conover, son of Van Rensselaer. Until their recent deaths, my mother's brother, Leander, and his wife, Beulah, continued to live on the Mason Road farm. It was they who gave me the family business papers on which this story is based.

The bottom lands between these Conover Hills had very rich sandy soil, ideal for raising high quality seed potatoes. In 1912 and for three years later my father, Almon Preston Fisher, raised these desirable potatoes and sold them to the seed potato dealers in Fishers. My mother and I would drive the horse and buggy the two and a half miles from the Fisher homestead on Main Street, Fishers, to Turk Hill to eat a noon meal with my father, and I romped over the hills. A forest of chestnut trees grew there. Nutting time was a memorable social event at our house. A wagon load of guests was driven to the woods to gather the abundant chestnuts and then back home for a good country dinner at noon. The barns and cedar rail corrals which I remember have all vanished. The business office and residence once owned by Van Rensselaer Conover is now the remodeled home of Mr. and Mrs. John McNulty at 647 Thayer Road.

The Mysterious
Dancing Cane

Any wooden cane that would dance by itself without the aid of some electrical or mechanical device or other means has to be mysterious. It must have been levitation, but how?

The carved cane that my father, Almon Preston Fisher, used created much speculation at house parties and dances at the beginning of this century and was nothing more than a witchhazel sapling.

Perhaps Witchhazel has some unusual properties which made possible the queer antics of this stick of wood. After all, the distillate of the bark of this bush was widely used as a remedy by the Indians and pioneers for bruises, sprains, etc.

Long years ago I first heard about the strange attributes of this cane from my neighbor, James Sullivan. I took it to him to have him show me how it worked. The only person he knew, he said, who could make it dance was my father. He would hold the cane between his knees and spin it with his open palms and then spread them apart and the cane would dance like it was supported in an electric field. This cane would bounce and sway with music and resonating sounds. What makes me sad is that there is no one else who could do the magic with this cane. Therefore, it can only be enjoyed for its fine carving.

A Confession

Vandalism, or harming someone, was never a part of my way of having fun. If a practical joke was involved, it was best to act alone, never letting anyone know, except my family, and thus I was never a suspect.

My one big act of impropriety was in 1924 when I burned a fiery cross; it upset and scared the whole community. The newspapers were full of frightful stores which told of the steady advance northward of the growing membership of the Ku Klux Klan. It seemed like a long time to wait for the excitement about the Klan to reach our area and, I thought, as a teenager, why not speed up the hysteria?

On our farm was a high hill overlooking the valley and Fishers. This was the best spot to burn a cross to make people believe that the dreaded Ku Klux Klan had at last arrived. I had to be sure that if I went to all that trouble that the blaze would be seen. I asked my brother, Francis, to stand by our house and spread the alarm the moment he saw the blaze. He did, but in the excitement he fainted, which created problems. Neighbor children, who happened by at the moment, saw him fall and saw the fire, so they spread the alarm.

The seven o'clock train had just arrived from Rochester and my mother got off amidst all the running around and excitement. The firebell rang and men ran for the Model T fire truck, which headed west not knowing where they were going. On the way

123

they saw the cross burning with no way to get to it.

Men stopped by our barn to question me. They saw that I was halfway through milking our cow and besides, how could I have crossed the creek at the foot of the hill? Therefore, since I could not have done it, the Klan had to be announcing their arrival. My interrogators didn't know that I had previously half-milked the cow and crossed the creek both ways at a little known dry spot.

Everyone but my family believed that the dreaded Klan had at last arrived this far north. Five automobile loads of people drove to Victor to see what Father Kelly could do about it. Bill O'Brien telegraphed a story to the Rochester newspaper telling about the arrival of the Ku Klux Klan.

I kept myself scarce, but the next morning I looked uptown and saw many housewives standing on their walks with brooms in their hands after sweeping, just speculating. That morning many people dared to climb the hill to investigate the situation. They found the remains of the burned cross, several coins and hoof prints of horses all around. The coins happened to have been lost by the visitors themselves, and the hoof prints were the horses using the rented pasture. The whole spoof worked better than I could have anticipated. I have never laughed as hard before or since.

The Procrastination Tree

The day that Governor Thomas E. Dewey broke the ground for the great New York Thruway was a momentous occasion for Western New York. The event took place on October 25, 1946, at the intersection of Main Street Fishers and Route 96.

The area for the ceremonies had been cleared of brush and high weeds and a portable flag-draped bandstand was brought in for the speakers. Another stand held the players of the Genesee Valley Band and those of the Victor Central School. Earth moving machinery was lined up for the big send-off of the project by the Governor. A fifteen man detail of State Police came early to handle the traffic assisted by the Fishers firemen with their new truck.

By 12:30 several thousand people had assembled to hear the four speakers, of which I was one. Governor Dewey gave the dedicatory address and before he spoke, he thanked me for the local hospitality expressed by the large banner welcoming him to Fishers, which I had placed above the crowd facing him.

I needed a pole opposite the speakers' platform upon which to suspend one end of the banner, the other end was on the nearby telephone pole. I had cut a willow pole down by our creek and dragged it behind my car to the site. I should have taken the pole down right away, but instead kept saying "I'll do it tomorrow." Time went on and on and then I discovered that the pole had taken root and was growing into a tree. Twenty years later the Thruway Authority named it the Governor Thomas E. Dewey Tree and gave instructions to maintain it as a landmark. At about the same time the former governor happened to be in Rochester, and when I told him the story, he exclaimed, "Oh, my gosh!"

The "Procrastination Tree"
Later renamed by the New York Thruway Authority. Top of the original pole shows in the top center of the tree.

The
Fish
Horn
Alarm and other stories by J. Sheldon Fisher.

Privy Art, Happy Makers and the Ghost of Eliza O'Brien. Guarding Troop Trains, the Fairy Farm and Cannonading the Thruway. These and many more tales from J. Sheldon Fisher continue his excellent presentation in the style of *The Groaning Tree*

Watch for it in your favorite bookstore
or order direct from the publisher:

Empire State Books
PO Box 299
Interlaken, New York 14847

The Author

In 1940 J. Sheldon Fisher and his wife Lillian purchased Valentown Hall and established the Valentown Museum to house his collection that is as diverse as his interests. Iroquoiria, Military, Scientific, Folk Lore, Genealogical—all attract the curiosity and investigation of the man "Hiawasees," the name given him by the Seneca Indians in 1964 at the time of his adoption by the Heron clan. It means "the eagle who gathers news and history" and it is an appropriate handle for Fisher who has spent most of his life gathering, chronicling and preserving the history of western New York.

Professionally, he helped build the renown archaeological collection of the Rochester Museum and Science Center and became the first County Historian on Ontario County. Always active as a volunteer in community organizations, he was a founder of the Rochester Genealogical Society and the Fishers' Fire Department as well as reconstituting a Civil War cavalry regiment, the First New York Dragoons.

Shortly before his 80th birthday, in the summer of 1987, he was honored as a primary influence in the 42 year campaign that led to the dedication of Ganondagan, the first New York State Historic Site devoted to Indian culture.

The Groaning Tree is his first publication of folk tales. It is filled with memories that show human nature at its best.